THE BIG R
of a
SUCCESSFUL
BUSINESS

FAUNTEEWRITES

A Faunteewrites Imprint
By Faunteewrites Limited, since 2012.
www.fauntee.com

Published by Faunteewrites Limited

© Emeka Anyanwu 2016.

The Big R of A Successful Business.

Emeka Anyanwu asserts the moral right to be identified as the author of this work in accordance with the copyright, designs and patents act 1988.

A CIP catalogue record for this book is available from the British Library.

ISBN: 9780993041754

CONTENTS

ACKNOWLEDGEMENT

I would like to thank the almighty God for giving me the inspiration and strength to put my thoughts together.
Also I would like to thank Mr Kevin Reddy for his kindness and insight in discovering the content for this book. Without your honest discussion with me, sharing your ideas, this book may not have been born.

DEDICATION

To my wife, Faustina Anyanwu and my mother, Helen Anyanwu.
You are the two most important women in my life.
Thank you for your love and kindness.
This is for you.

SECTION A

I can fly; with my mind. **Emeka Anyanwu**

FOREWORD:

BACKGROUND

In writing my experiences, I'm not passing any judgement. Nor am I imposing my own values and opinions.

The greatest conquest in life is that of the mind. This book will not only lead you through the journey of business success but, also through joy and happiness. Your prosperity depends on your ability to maximise your talent, which has more to do with an internal mindset, rather than external actions.

You must see yourself as a leader. This is the first and the most important thing.

"The most common way people give up power is by thinking they don't have any," according to Alice Walker.

"Everybody is a genius. But if you judge a fish by its ability to climb a tree, it will live its whole life believing it is stupid." **Albert Einstein**

Background brings a masterpiece to life like no other value. Not only does it aesthetically enhance its properties, but it resonates and captures people's imaginations—more so than any other embedded qualities or signatures.

To appreciate a masterpiece, one needs to step into the background to understand the context: the relationship a brilliant work has with its backdrop. The dramatic backdrop could have hidden information about the masterpiece. You cannot separate a work from its backdrop.

Your background defines you: your personality, your presence, your context, and your facade. If one is isolated from their environment, one becomes impotent, out of touch, and unproductive. Powerful judges do not only look at the body of evidence. They move further to look at the context, background or the circumstance of each case before reaching a conclusion. Regardless of the perspectives of the involved parties.

Sometimes this backdrop is invisible or hidden. That means you have to ask, seek and knock before you can walk in through its threshold. Look at trees with their roots in the soil; think of fish in the great waters and birds of the air. All is dependent on the environment. One would ask, where do humans belong? Our environment is not visible, and neither is it the one society foisted on us. Our environment is the presence of God and forms the backdrop. The man who discovers himself has also discovered God. That's why humans are inseparable from our God. Nothing can separate us from God. Our background is that of power, love and sound mind. This reflects where human power lies. *This is what gives one strong sense of mission.* Nothing can resist human will. Therefore, begin to avoid all impossibilities in your life as you read this book.

God has given us powerful minds to create our present and a better future; to bring joy and happiness into our lives and that of others. Great inventors and entrepreneurs of all ages relied on God through their minds to overpower all challenges and obstacles. From Leonardo Da Vinci, to Albert Einstein,Steve Jobs and Bill Gates and now this generation of Tech leaders such as Mark Zuckerberg. All of these people understood and appreciated the power of the mind.

What one hasn't conceived first in the mind cannot be built in the physical world. More than 75% of any work is first created in the mind. No wonder Albert Einstein said,

"If I'm given an hour to save the world, I would use 59 minutes to define the problem and take 1 minute to solve it."

Whatever you're able to define is already achieved. You can become whatever you want as long as you know what that is and have learnt the way to achieve that. To create a house, the architect must first conceive and design it in their mind. We can't stress enough the power of the mind. Unless we understand its tremendous power, and take leadership responsibility for our own personal life, you cannot change the situation for the better.

N.B. What the mind of man can conceive, the will of a man achieves!

One can see that the power of personal leadership to create a vision for one's future. This is in the mind. The willpower is rooted in the value and meaning you attach to your goals; the goals rooted in the vision in your mind. In Jim Steele, Martin Coburn and Colin Hiles' book 'Break through to Peak Performance,' there's a saying: "All our goals, all our dreams and desires are nothing but the vehicles for fulfilling our values. They are symbols we can see in front of us like an icon and identity. If we become disconnected with our values, then we lose motivation."

What we appreciate is what we value. What we value is what we respect. What we respect is what we attract. This gives birth to **'The Big "R" Of A Successful Business.'** Having known that God endowed humans with His spirit, this part of God in us forms a formidable background and deserves 'RESPECT'. Under this backdrop, we have this concept: **Respect for oneself, Respect for others, and Respect for products and services,** if one wants to achieve success with grace and ease. The true currency of business is not money but **Respect**. It is never weakness, it's rather strength.

The objective of this book is to reveal to one their own. Once you understand who you are through your talent then, you can pursue excellence and meet up with your own personal values and goals. In my terms, this is success. How one measures up to the best of themselves. This book is totally based on *'hands on experience,'* not a fantasy of bypassing work.

Given this fact, our willpower helps to create and achieve anything which comes from the mind. The tragedy is, the same mind harbours a formidable enemy within it. According to Timothy Gallwey: *"The opponent within one's head is more formidable than the one on the other side of the net."* This presents humans with a huge challenge: An enemy within their mind. This is the reason 80% of work in the **'The Big 'R' Of A successful business.'** is centred on the mind. It's where all battles are fought and won. And it is for this fact that the mind is worth exploring.

Look at what the mind can do: I uploaded messages every week in YouTube prior to Xmas 2015. At first, the video which I tried uploading wasn't going to load. I thought it was network problem.

I left it for a while then checked it after a day and nothing was loaded. This continued like that; the final one happened on the new year. I tried to upload and nothing worked. I got the same result. I left it again for two days to no avail. At three days, nor at one week did anything occur. I showed it to my colleague and he could not come up with any reasonable advice. In my mind, I thought it was YouTube's technical problem. Their staff may not have been back from holiday.

With a different mindset, I decided to go contrary to what my mind was telling me. I decided to delete most of the pictures on my phone to give it another go. Instantly, the new trial worked out. I should have troubleshooted the problem first, but I fell victim once again to my mind.

Most of us are victims to a lot of inhibiting negative thoughts that trudge around in our mind. We are being held hostage by irrelevant things we constantly think of. These exaggerate things. It prevents us from pursuing our goals, dreams and vision. Until you learn to change and internalise new ways of doing things, there'll not be any possibility of realising our potentials. This is an example of the feeling that usually make one believe their life is shaped by forces beyond their control. Don't allow your mind to play that game on you. Above all, life is a journey. Once you know your purpose and destination, half of your journey has been made. Few people attain great lives, mainly because it's easier to settle for the least.

"Our problems are manmade – therefore they can be solved by man. And can be as big as he wants. No problem of human destiny is beyond human beings. Man's reason and spirit have often solved the seemingly unsolvable – and we believe they can do it again." **John F. Kennedy**

See every challenge as an opportunity.

The future belongs to those who believe in the beauty of dreams.
Eleanor Roosevelt

The Big 'R' Of A Successful Business demonstrates that successful businesses Run on a principle of RESPECT. Whatever we have is what we have RESPECT for. To be successful one has to pass through water and fire.

CHAPTER 1

INTRODUCTION

Every word is an action.

I'm not passing any judgement, nor am I imposing my own values and opinions. We can't be friends with everyone but we can be friendly with everyone.

Everything we do in life is all about relationships. When it comes to business relationships, **RESPECT** is the most important ingredient. There is an obligation to return favour to another, which has made Respect a powerful tool in all relationships.

RESPECT is finding value in what you have. Respect isn't only about treating people nice; it is about internally seeing that power they have to do their very best. That is what helps the company to succeed.

The aim of 'The Big R of a successful business' is to show how the concept of **Respect for oneself, people, products and services,** can lead one to be successful in business. What you affirm is what you attract. If you have Respect for people, you give them the right products and services. **Whatever people have RESPECT for comes to them.** I spent a bit of time on the foreword to explain the importance of a human's background as that of God.

Transform yourself by continuously renewing your mind.
St. Paul, Romans 12:2

Remember, humans have the capacity to achieve everything in which they set their mind. This is my philosophy. Nothing is impossible. If you can visualise yourself doing something, then you got the talent inside of you to do it. You have all the power in the universe within you!

All wars are fought in the mind; therefore, prepare to renew your mind every moment as you have heard from the great apostle and the founder of christianity. You can't rest on your laurel. **Anything that is not for others is meaningless. All we do originates from and revolves around this law: 'Love thy neighbour.' This is why RESPECT is at the heart of all we do.** Respect is the true currency of business, not money. Establish a quality relationship and see how things move quickly.

It beggars belief that some humans do not know that they are children of God. Therefore, there are little gods capable of achieving everything through the **Respect for Oneself, People and Products and Services.** Hence, **"The Big 'R' Of A Successful Business."**

It is not the size of the dog but the fight in a dog. **Unknown**

One morning, I was having a breakfast with my wife. In attempt to poke her, I called her Mrs. Junket. Unexpectedly, she turned around and started laughing at me. She then said, "Yes, I am Mrs Junket. Guess what that makes you? Mr Junket."

Instantly I realised that whatever you throw at someone comes back to you immediately. And both of us ended up laughing it off. I was amazed at how she seemed unfazed. This is life. Your thoughts and words come back to you; they make you who you are. They create your reality. So, if you don't treat yourself with **Respect**, then others will not treat you with **Respect**. This is where the power lies: **Good health, wealth and passion are all in the frequency of RESPECT.**

As our body's organs are connected to function, so is **Respect** for oneself, people and products. They are connected to form a business success. How you respect and interact with employees, customers and suppliers affects not only the image of the company but sales. Businesses that don't change their culture will soon see themselves being passed over as more flexible, creative, innovative, and adaptable competitors move in to take their position.

The Big 'R' Of A Successful Business" wouldn't have been written if I hadn't shown Respect to my colleague, Mr.Kevin Reddy. First and foremost, I was not planning to write a book. All I was doing was writing an article to be published on C. Hub magazine's Website on the topic: "How To Turn Your Hobby Into a Business." I decided to ask Kevin for contributions. Little did I know that my colleague had lots of insight. He is well-grounded in a field of which I was treading. Instantly I knew Kevin had given me a great idea for a book. This is an invaluable gift. The seed of success has been sown, not only in my heart but in the hearts of others that will read **"The Big 'R' Of A Successful Business."**

This illustrates that, **'Respect'** is your power in business. Don't underestimate its power when it comes to making you successful or putting millions in your bank account. The person you ignore might be holding the key to your wealth and as an entrepreneur; you obviously need him. Besides, "You reap what you sow." If you disrespect people, people will disrespect you. **One of the most fundamental laws of human nature: we reap what we sow. If you respect people, people will respect you.**

Business opens doors of opportunity for people. There is no love greater than that of opening of doors of opportunity for your people.

Opportunity is more powerful even than conquerors and prophets.
Benjamin Disraeli

Remember that your background defines you—not your physical background. It is the internal that determines external. This is your root. The background and image we have is that of God. So, impossibilities are to be avoided. This awareness gives rise to the 'R' in this book. Technically, the knowledge for **Respect** inspired us to start our business and to publish. C. Hub magazine aimed at giving creative Africans their voice in global branding.

Respect is what gives one strong sense of mission.

The **Respect** we have for ourselves and others was translated into producing the best quality magazine for our audience. We hold our customers in high repute and we couldn't be careless as to produce a substandard product. This is not in line with our image, beliefs and values. The way we value and respect ourselves is the way we value and respect others.

Remember, business is not difficult. Rather, it is people that make it difficult. Business leaders identified that more than 75% of critical business issues are on the relational side, rather than on finance and technical side. Relationships between humans are ruled by emotions. Understanding people, especially customers, is the key. There is no business without customers.

The true currency of business is not money but RESPECT. When we have Respect for our relationships, 75% of the problem is knocked off.
As noted by Franklin D. Roosevelt:

> *The most important single ingredient in the formula of success is knowing how to get along with people.*

One of the most fundamental laws of human nature: we reap what we sow. If you respect people, people will respect you.

Why must a person be successful in their work?

We all have assignments handed to us by God, our creator. This a special assignment for which we are given talent; this is where our sense of joy and happiness is fulfilled. Above all, other humans are waiting and are dependent on this special and unique assignment to be carried out. The only way to completely understand oneself is to understand others, and that gives us courage to succeed.

> *"To each there comes in their lifetime a special moment when they are figuratively tapped on the shoulder and offered the chance to do a very special thing, unique to them and fitted to their talents. What a tragedy if that moment finds them unprepared or unqualified for that which could have been their finest hour."* **Winston Churchill**

We're created to be successful. It is said that a man who did not use his talent was stripped of his one talent and given to someone who had 5. Besides, if we fail to be successful, nature will definitely conspire against us.

For one to be successful in business they must satisfy this simple and plain test for **Respect**: They are the fundamental pillars of a successful business. Great businesses run on the principle of **Respect** because, whatever we **RESPECT**, comes to us.

1. **Respect for self**
2. **Respect for people**
3. **Respect for one's products and services**

The Big R of a Successful business re-assesses oneself, people, products and services to extract that energy. It harnesses enthusiasm, in which we have left untapped for centuries. I like to take the holistic approach to business.

The Big R of a successful business is a concept that uses the principle of RESPECT. It establishes the key to a successful business. *Success is confidence and enthusiasm developed as a result of the understanding acquired through knowledge and its application.*

RESPECT, as a principle in business success, runs very deep in the inner self, people, products and services. Respect to oneself is the essential spark. It leads first to respect for people and then to products. One who does not have respect for himself cannot have respect for another; no one gives what they do not have. One who does not have respect for people hardly produces a brand that connects or resonates with the people. By paying attention to these relationships—we can confidently accomplish our purposes, goals, mission and vision to become successful. This is not only effective in business, but in other field of endeavours. This is not mindset; it's beyond how one sees oneself, others and the world. Again, this is not a case of personality that rests on behaviour and responses.

It's vital for one to have complete understanding of themselves. One who is unable to conquer themselves cannot conquer another. All battles start in the mind and, once your mind is conquered—you cannot go anywhere. All the battles are won and lost in the mind. The root cause of our despair is in our mind. This is where the Respect for self comes from before it spreads to people, products and services.

Many do not have respect for their talent, gifts, words and their abilities.

What is the first thing you do if you want to win big time? Certainly you have to reclaim your mind and re-educate yourself to believe in yourself. Believe in your vision and have that mentality of 'dominion' given to you by your creator – God. The blueprint of success.

Our mind is the seat of power. This is a place where the journey starts and ends. The big choice in life is made only in the mind. Choice is power, and exercising that choice is the energy. Many do not like to make this choice because it involves change which in turn involves risk and sacrifice. There's no change without risk.

The second step is; delivering this vital energy extracted from our mind to the people. That is, bringing that value to the market. Archbishop Desmond Tutu said: **"A person is a person through another person."** Engaging with the people becomes the key here. If you go to the people with trust and confidence, in turn they will give you trust and confidence. How can you get the trust when we have no respect for them? It is said: **"business is not difficult, it is people who are."** One has to understand people's psychology if they have to engage them. Good attitude comes into play here. The attitude we choose determines how successful we become.

If we adopt a negative attitude towards our environment, you've already lost the plot. As we'll be seeing in the subsequent pages on attitude. Jesse Owen is one of the greatest Athletes of all time. He upstaged and subverted prejudice at home and in Berlin during Hitler's era to win four gold medals in 1936.

He said, "There is something that can happen to every athlete and every human being. The instinct to slack off, to give less than your best, the instinct to hope you can win through luck or through your opponent not doing his best. Instead of going to your limit and passing your limit where victory is always found. Defeating those negative instincts that are out to defeat us is the difference between winning and losing and we face that battle everyday of our lives."

The third test is; the respect for the products and services. This is a test for distinction. A product does not stand out without distinction. As a result, obviously it will not sell. Having extracted this energy from our mind, and delivered it to the people, the question then becomes: What is this energy?

One's products and services are the expression of one's values, thoughts, beliefs and uniqueness. These are what one cannot separate from themselves. For instance, C. Hub magazine embodies the values, uniqueness, thoughts and beliefs of which we subscribe: excellence and authenticity. The value one has for oneself transcends to the value they have for people, leading to the quality of the product they produce. The values the products express must connect with people. "No one gives what they don't have."

There is a correlation between how we render our services and how we think that make most employers like Goldman and Sachs, Citi and UBS aim at employing the best. "The best are best at maximising smallness." A vessel is known by the sound, whether it be cracked or not. People are known by the products and services which they offer to others. Your products and services do say a lot about you. It is very difficult for one to offer excellent products and services to people if they do not have respect for them. Besides, it's very difficult to promote a product one does not believe in.

Marketplace is crowded with products and services. The last thing one can think of is to have products or services that are not unique and are not of good value. We publish this magazine in the genre that is highly competitive. If you do not produce an excellent and quality magazine, you are in for a long haul. The demand for your product will drop, putting you out of business. There's no way you can produce the best product without that passion, interest and bonding. The respect I'm saying here is this: bond and passion exist between brand owners and products. Psalm:(139:14) says: We are fearfully and wonderfully made. Extracting that similar feeling of painstaking feeling you have before you produce the product.

My second daughter's birthday gift was a bike. In fact, that was her wish. On Saturday, she and her mum came back from author, Ibitola's Insight of an author show. I was lying on the bed a bit tired. She walked in with smiles and said, "Hello Dad, when are we going for the bike ride?" I smiled back without saying a word. Standing closer, she said: "You promised today." I laughed and told her: "Dan, can you come back in few hours. I'm a bit tired." Then, she left—only to turn up again in less than 30 minutes to remind me that it was time. "Dad, it's time," she said with enthusiasm. Without much thought, I discharged her: "Don't worry Dan. I'll be with you soon." And she left leaving me wondering: "Am really in trouble today if I don't keep to this promise? She is so excited and passionate about this.

"Go on! Go on!" She could barely pedal the bike. She was shaking; goosebumps and fear swept her feet off the pedal. "Get on!" I said to her as I gave a trust to the bike. With smiles and enthusiasm, she applied pressure on the pedal. She made a full 360-cycle, and was about to make another one when she landed on the ground. I heard eruption of laughter from kids playing in the park as she looked up to see them, becoming shy. She grabbed the bike, breathed in, charged up and continued. Unbelievably, she didn't let people's remarks and fear stop her from getting on her bike. Failure is not what stops us from living our dreams. What stops us is quitting. Never let failure stop you. Danielle did not quit. She was quite focused, passionate and determined to achieve her goal. After that day we continued, and today she can ride with boldness and confidence.

In a nutshell, business is like riding a bike. This scenario illustrates the guiding principles in business.

Success like in competition is not luck, you must understand the rule of the game and be able to apply it for you to win.

The Big 'R' Of A Successful Business demonstrates that successful businesses Run on a principle of RESPECT.

THE BENEFITS OF "THE BIG R OF A SUCCESSFUL BUSINESS."

+ The Big 'R' Of A Successful Business' teaches you how to use your power and energy to transform your work and leisure into a successful business. Our goal is to put you at your rightful place. Become the most powerful brand.

Benjamin Barber, an eminent and powerful sociologist said, "I don't divide the world into the weak and strong, or the successes and failures. I divide the world into the learners and non learners."

+ Success is the ability of one to improve on what one already have and to make their life better, this book goes to the core of human success – **the ability to learn.**

'The Big R Of A Successful Business,' provides the vital context for learning how to be great in life and to become a successful entrepreneur. Since we can learn everything in life. Why not be a learner rather than a lament?

+ It helps you to build that huge financial independence. It will help you to realise your potentials.
+ It provides the insights and expertise which we need to be great people and manifest that glory of God in us.
+ It helps you to build work and life balance. You don't want to continue on the same trajectory that paints the same landscape of one being powerless.
+ It provides you the strength to stand up for things you believe to be fair and just for all humans.

+ The Big R of a successful business motivates you to give your best. It starts with your state of mind: respecting oneself, respecting people, products or services.
+ It would be naive for anyone to assume that success in business will definitely slot into their positions without effective plan and work. This illusion has been sold to us for centuries.
+ Identifying the moving parts (and non-moving parts) is crucial in life, as well as in business.
+ It helps one develop and tap into our intellectual powers to create a powerful future for them and the next generation

Having **RESPECT** for oneself will give you key to access the huge potential in people, products and services. It helps to generate wealth required to achieve your purposes in life.

+ The Big R provides you with the insight needed to fill the gap between past decisions and future intentions. This will lift huge number of people out of poverty.
+ It provides us with the hard skills needed to run our businesses now and in the future.
+ You will never be powerless with the Big R. You cease to be a victim in any circumstance in your life: we become leaders and managers. There is no growth if there's no effective management.
+ It helps you to think globally and to make sure your brands resonate on a global level.
+ It provides one with the necessary strategy to get things done on time and to budget.
+ Business is about relationship. It helps you change your attitude and habits. It gives you the ability to love what you do for life.
+ Engaging oneself with 'The Big R Of A Successful Business' will make you thrive and excel. It will teach you the principles of top performance. You should not play second fiddle in your area of gifting.
+ The concept will spur you to come out of your comfort zone. It will engage your most powerful tool—your brain.
+ There is no guarantee of a job for life anymore. With knowledge of The Big R Of A Successful Business, you not only become your own boss but the initiator of change itself.

+   When you understand The Big R of a Successful Business, then you see change as opportunity and no longer a problem. "One gives freely, yet grows all the richer; another withholds what he should give, and only suffers want." Proverbs 11:24

The more you give the more you receive. The more you give out your talent, the richer you become.

RESPECT = SUCCESS

"For many are called, but few are chosen." Matt 22:14

We're created to be highly successful. But we have to learn the art as Dan was learning her bike riding. Birds are created to fly, yet they have to learn how to fly. It is a journey of self-discovery: courage to fly and successfully land a jumbo jet without being trained. You must believe in yourself. See every challenge as an opportunity! Many will embark on a journey of success. Only a few will make it at the finish line. Unless one brands themselves, they become the many.

The only way we can fulfil our original purpose is for us to be successful. If you have **RESPECT** for your purpose, then you will accomplish it. Success is in our DNA. Competition is also in our blood. We have the greatest power in our hands. That power of choice. That free will. The choice to start your own business rather than working for another. Since profit is better than wages. Unless we have **Respect** for all these, they just don't make any meaning. **Anything that is not for others is meaningless. All we do originates from and revolves around this law: 'Love thy neighbour.' This is why RESPECT is at the heart of all we do. Whatever we have RESPECT for comes to us.**

Apply these skills in your business today, you will be amazed at the rate of changes in your returns.

You simply cannot fail; you only have to learn from your mistakes. Mistakes, small and big, often provide the best learning opportunities. We are born to be extremely successful.

Never ever quit; this validates it. If Dan had quit when she failed, that would have been the end of her dream of riding a bike. Again, look at her attitude and recovery rate.

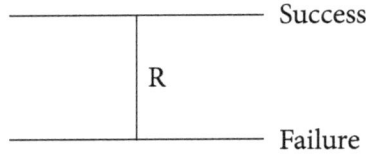

```
 ────────────┬──────────── Success
             │
             │ R
             │
 ────────────┴──────────── Failure
```

R = Respect: finding value in what you have. Respect is the cornerstone of what we do. Anything we don't have Respect for, we do not value.

> *Respect is how to treat everyone, not just those you want to impress.*
> **Richard Branson**

Both success and failure started with intent and purpose. The difference is, however, that failure ignores **Respect 'R',** while **Success** takes **Respect** onboard. What you **Respect,** you attract.

When one takes on the philosophy of Respect: oneself, people, and product. Then they rise to the level of success. The real thing that moves business is Respect. Knowing how to get along with people is so powerful in business. Remember people choose who they want to do business with—people they know, people they love, and people they trust. **One of the most fundamental laws of human nature: we reap what we sow. If you respect people, people will respect you.**

Success is more real than failure if you love and believe in what you do.

Success is more of a state of mind than what you're seeing.

Success is real and a means to an end. Like I said earlier, we are like aircrafts designed and built to fly. All what we need has been provided. All this depends on the pilot. **God created us to be successful. Everything has been provided to us. We are complete. Everything else depends on the individual to make the choice.**

Above all, one would like businesses to be based on ethical principles not by bullying, intimidation and ego to establish oneself.

When we put down all the core elements of a successful business together they boiled down to one word: RESPECT. A successful person understands the difference in people, seasons, time, location and products.

Business at any level has it's challenges. You must constantly refine and reflect on your judgement, according to St. Paul, one of the greatest minds.

You must see yourself as a leader and your mission is to bring change to the world. Every effective and successful leader is supposed to change the landscape, but not to allow the landscape to change them. If you do, it means you had no mission in the first place. You are not a leader.

If you want to change the world, then you must change yourself. It's said, "The best way to make your dreams come true is to wake up."

Success is a word that virtually has been in human mind from the time of creation. Increase and multiply. Success is real, and as soon we are born we are on that way. Success not only gives you influence, but also determines how well you are relative to your personal purpose in life. Success is a personal thing. One cannot compare themselves with another because you do not know their personal assignment, purpose and vision in life. Your success in an area of gifting will give you influence in life. This is why talent is highly important if you must be successful. "Success is not a pursuit. Success is, as a result, obedience to laws," according to Dr Myles Munroe.

For me, your success depends on your ability to maximise your talent. To maximise on your talent ,you must work on yourself more than you work on your job. The first place to start is one's mind.

PERSONAL SUCCESS

Real success in life has to be between you and your God. He is the one that gave your personal assignment, purpose and talent. You might be a top performer when assessed with others, yet not successful. On the other hand, people see you as mediocre while you are successful. The concept of success is relative to the purpose for which you are created in the first place. It is up to you and your God to determine if you are successful or not. It's never up to people to determine if you are successful or not. The key to measuring success in life is to discover the purpose for which you are created – original assignment. Your success in life is measured by what you are created to do, compared to what you've done. You are the one that defines success for yourself but never others.

Fulfilment and completion of the original assignment is success, no wonder Jesus said: "It is finished." St. Paul, the founder of Christianity, echoed the same thing: "I have finished my race,.."

"Everything hinges on gift."

What is it are giving? Are you giving with your heart, mind and soul?

Let's examine these two scenarios that illustrated success. The first case in point was played out hugely during Cain and Abel. Cain and Abel offered sacrifice to God. Abel had respect and offered a perfect sacrifice to God. Cain, the elder brother, had no Respect. He offered a foolish, rotten and an unbefitting sacrifice to God. Another story goes this way: two people went into the temple to pray. One was Republican and another the Pharisee. The Republican was successful because his was Respectful and honest. He made an intelligent prayer. The Pharisee, who had no Respect for his neighbour, prayed a dangerous prayer and was unsuccessful. These two stories illustrated to us what it means to be successful. How lack of Respect in our attitude can prevent us from being successful. Success involves a form of exchange and engagement that leads to unique joy and happiness. We can only be successful if we have Respect for our calling and our gifts. Success is about what we aim to achieve and your ability to distinguish yourself from the rest. Success is the result of your hard work. It is earned; don't take it as luck. According to Robert Holden: **"My success is my gift to the world."**

Ideally, success is what you have done or achieved in regards your purpose in life. You might achieve a lot in other things in life, but if it is not your purpose, then you still feel unfulfilled and unhappy. From those two illustrations, you can see why some come out successfully in business and while some come crashing out. Being successful is not about giving customers services, but rather it's about having respect for clients and customers. You have to provide better service that's distinct from what your competitors. There are many products and services out there. What makes yours different is the key. The question becomes this: what are you offering to your customers? What kind of products and services are you rendering? Is there any Respect for customers and clients? Is there a deep sense of commitment? What kind of mindset does one have? These are questions that form the underlying reasons why this book was written to set you on the road to success.

...You become what you think about most, but you also attract what you think about most. **John Assaraf**

God has given us power to dominate, He has instructed the universe to listen and obey in order to accomplish God's purpose and plan for us. "Whatever you bind on earth, heaven will bind it." It means heaven will listen. Nothing will be impossible for you if you have faith. This is authority. This is power. Whatever we thought and declare, the universe will obey and the gate of hell cannot prevail against this. This is why our thoughts and words should be extremely guarded. You can speak your word into existence. Our dominant thoughts in our lives are our reality. In this way, God has given us power to think and say out what we want to become. You can have, do, or be anything you want. This is the kind of enormous power we have; yet it beggars beliefs that the majority still blame others for their fate and destiny. Your destiny is in your hands. Your power of thoughts is in your hands and now becomes what you want to be.

Moaning and blaming people is counterproductive. By doing so, you're delivering this vital power to the person who you are blaming for your misfortune. When you complain, you are attracting the same thing that you are complaining about through law of attraction. When you listen intently to someone complaining, your focus turns to their complaints. You try to sympathise with them, while you are effectively playing out scenarios in your mind. What do you think the law of attraction will do? It will just reflect them back to the person. Evil to them that think evil! Negative mindset only begets negativity. You are the author of your own success.

What is the mindset of the one given one talent in the Bible?

That of doubt and negativity.

What did he receive?

He received punishment. The only talent he had was taken away because he didn't invest it.

One's success depends on the law they know and understand. The majority of these laws do not let you off scot free on the basis that you don't know them. They will hit the person, gbam! They don't care whether you know them or not. Think of the law of gravity. If one disobeys the law, then they will hit the ground.

Remember, what you **Respect** is what you attract. It's attracted by virtue of images one's holding in their mind. This law of attraction is always forming one's entire life experience.

Every thought of yours is a real thing – a force.
Prentice Mulford (1834–1891)

If you want to be successful, then identify a problem to solve! It is through service that we become great. When Christ started his ministry, He went about looking for problems to solve using his gift of dominion. In the words of Martin Luther King Jr: "Everybody can be great because everybody can serve." Here he linked greatness with service. Find a problem which you can solve in the world using your gifts, talent and insight. This is why one has to have **Respect** for their talent. And that includes honing that talent to become the best you can be. Your success in life depends on your insights and laws you **Respect** and obey. When you know these laws, you know the power you have, know the God in you. Furthermore, you know your potentials. Immediately you will start to manifest the Glory of God within you. Impossibilities become a thing of past.

Do you know why nothing is impossible to you?

This is because your background is that of God. God is within you, and you live in the presence of God. You are practically and spiritually God and you're bigger than Satan. Of course you are a child of Almighty God.

Success in life is as a result of obedience to the law. **Dr Myles Munroe**

Do not let this Book of the Law depart from your mouth: meditate on it day and night, so that you may be careful to do everything written in it. Then you will be prosperous and successful. **Joshua 1:8**

God has enshrined His Law in all His creation, that everything works based on principles and Laws. Once you understand and obey these laws the universe will listen and obey. Heaven will do what you want.

What most people don't understand is that a thought has a frequency. We can measure a thought. And so, if you're thinking that thought over and over and over again, if you're imagining in your mind having that brand new car, having the money that you need, building that company, finding your soulmate...if you're imagining what that looks like, you're emitting that frequency on a consistent basis. **John Assaraf**

When we meditate, we are sending out thoughts that have frequency. They attract things and these things are sent back to the source. Remember that you are the source. They will all come back to you. That's why if one thinks evil, evil comes to them. What you sow is what you reap.

Whatever you asked in my name, you shall have it." according to Jesus Christ. "Therefore I tell you, whatever you ask for in prayer, believe that you have received it, and it shall be yours. **Mark 11:24**

The reason many are not living out their dreams and in abundance is that they don't have faith. They don't truly believe in the law of attraction. And finally, they're constantly thinking about "what they don't want," rather than "what they truly want." For instance, many are always thinking out: "I don't want to be poor," instead of, "I want to be wealthy.

It is the mark of an educated mind to be able to entertain a thought without accepting it. **Aristotle**

The law of attraction is a law of nature. It is impersonal and it does not see good things or bad things. It is receiving your thoughts and reflecting back to you those thoughts as your life experience. The law of attraction simply gives you whatever it is you are thinking about.
The law of attraction is law of creation. Quantum physicists tell us that the entire universe emerged from thought! You create your life through your thoughts and law of attraction; every single person does the same. It doesn't just work if you know about it. It has always been working in your life and every other person's life throughout history. When you become aware of this great law, then you become aware of how incredibly powerful you are, to be able to THINK your life into existence. **The Secret by Rhonda Byrne**

This law of attraction is enshrined, that we often see them in the Bible.
    "Whatever you sow, so you shall reap."
    "Whatever a man thinketh, so It shall be."
    "Blessed are the merciful for they shall have mercy."
    To be successful, you've got to work smartly and that is knowledge of law. Knowing the law means working skillfully. With skill, success comes quickly.

As one progresses, and as success starts trickling in, you must be a prisoner of your own success. The day you start to liberate yourself of this good thing is the day you stop doing that thing which you love. The day you stop being passionate for your work is the day you have put your success in the reverse gear. Remember it's not what you know but how you come across. Do you aspire to be the best that you can be.

Success is about vision and strategy! One can't be successful unless they have **Respect** for what they do. The secret to success lies in making the best of what one has, and aligning this with what we want to achieve. Doing this is the most important thing if one wants to achieve genuine success. It means work, it means working smartly.

The only place where success comes before work is in a dictionary.
Vidal Sassoon

CHAPTER 2

RESPECT FOR INFORMATION AND KNOWLEDGE

People are not disturbed by events, but by the view they hold about them.
Epictetus, Stoic Philosopher

It's the view we hold that governs us rather than event, situation, or people. It is the thought that forms word; the words that form deeds; deeds form habits. We are what we constantly do. This is the reason these principles and beliefs are effective and powerful. Whatever we lack shows we don't have **Respect** for it. *If I want to look at anything, there's only one thing I check out for: The EUS(Essential Underlying Spirit) and this gives rise to RESPECT.*

The following principles will lock you in into the greatest and the most important powers in the universe:

Increase and Multiply. **God**

You find greatness when you maximise smallness. **Unknown**

PURPOSE

You are the salt of the earth; You are the light of the world. **Matthew 5:13**

Your purpose is your personal assignment. It is non-negotiable. And that's a problem you are created to solve. All we do on earth is about service to others. One must shine like a light. You are the light. A city built on the hill.

Purpose is the ground which you defend at any cost. It's something in you which you live for, and at the same time, risk your life for it. Without purpose, life is meaningless. Our life story has no meaning without it. It's your legacy. Your purpose is your food. Your purpose is your work. You must respect your purpose.

The principle of purpose is the most important principle in our lives, for it impacts all others. This is where one derives their personal assignment. Once you know your purpose and stick to it, you become more formidable and destined for success. You are no longer subject to manipulation and you can't collapse under any pressure. Regardless of any obstacles, you are bound to succeed.

Once I set my eyes on the objective, all obstacles must give way. **Unknown**

All obstacles disappear once you have purpose. Once you have identified something, the flip side is solution. Purpose is like a light; darkness disappears soon afterwards. Purpose separates us from the pack. People fail in life because they don't have a purpose. Your purpose is greater than your challenge. If I don't go after my purpose, then I've made myself a liar. If you don't go after your purpose, then you are worshipping a foreign god. For we are betrayed by what is false within us. The purpose of fish is to swim. God has built in swimming mechanism inside fish. Fish has identified its purpose. What does it do? The fish sticks to its unique purpose forever. In that same vein, the human who identifies his purpose must stick to it. This is why I said: "Your purpose is non-negotiable." Our supreme purpose is to serve God, but through the gift we've identified. My purpose is to serve God, but through writing, speaking and publishing.

Purpose creates success. It puts life into what we do. Everything God created has a purpose; and, everything starts with the 'WHY'.

It's yet to be proven if the '**why**' in all creation is equivalent to the Golden ratio = 1.6180339887, found in almost everything ever created. Great leaders start with **WHY** in everything they say and do. The difference now is do we have **Respect for our purpose?** Anything in which you don't respect, then you don't appreciate.

When you have a sense of purpose in life, it brings along with it a sense of meaning. This leads to achievement, satisfaction and well-being. When you know your purpose, you find courage to take risk. Why will you take risk if you don't know your purpose?

You are the beauty of the world; the salt of the earth. Without salt, things are tasteless and meaningless. You are the light of the world; a city built on a hill. You cannot be hidden. God has given you assignment and talent, and you can no longer hide them. You are beautiful, complete, and lack nothing. No one can undermine your value, nor attack your self-esteem because you are made perfect and beautiful. You are fitted for your assignment in the world. You must use your assignment and talent to make yourself happy, create an experience of joy, peace and love for people around you. Remember, everything is about love for others.

As you're reading **'This Big 'R' Of A Successful business,'** you are on the journey of starting your assignment—if you have not started already. If you are successful in your personal assignment—those tiny areas of personal gifting—then you are automatically successful in life. You are influential.

'You find greatness when you have maximised smallness.' This summarises the story of mustard seed. You are attached to God Almighty and nothing can separate you from this bond. No amount of challenges, obstacles or temptation can sway you or cut you off from this bond. The only one that can separate you from this strong bond is you. God has already set you to the part of success; He has told you to increase and multiply. You break the bond when you made a choice to listen to the wrong voices. But so long as you continue to renew yourself according to St. Paul, you're unstoppable.

Your personal assignment is the most important thing in your life. This gives us a strong sense of mission. In fact your purpose is non-negotiable.

Your assignment is the work for which God created you. Aristotle had shone light on this when he said:

> *Where the needs of the world and your*
> *talent crosses, there lies your vocation.*

Written in your heart, somehow your heart and intuition know what you will become. Rely on that tiny voice in your heart.

Instinct – the subconscious – is much more reliable than statistics.
Philip Carret

The thoughts of the righteous are right.
Proverb

The thoughts of the righteous are accurate because God put those thoughts inside of his heart.

Check out the thoughts of people like Abraham, Moses, Noah, David and Jesus Christ. The same are your thoughts if you're righteous. As a man thinketh so he shall be. This is written even in the sky and stars. You alone can say with clarity whether your current job is your calling. For some, teaching is their job and their work but to some it is not their job nor their work. The purpose of this book is to lead the reader to become himself. One can only love and respect themselves if they are able to become themselves. Until you respect yourself, it's impossible for another person to respect you. Start with yourself and the world will follow.

The tragedy of life is for one not to embark on his personal assignment; a salt losing its saltiness, lamp hidden under the table. You must be a light in the human heart. Shine! Shine! Shine! This is your purpose! This is clearly what separates you from the pack. This is what separates you from the crowd. I see my business as my personal assignment. One has a choice to ignore this or get real. Never work in a place where you cannot fulfil your dream or pave way to your purpose. You are born to accomplish something. This is your personal assignment. When you are locked onto this mission no turning back. Fear becomes irrelevant. Fear does not matter anymore.

Your personal assignment shows you the right turns; the direction that is right. It tells you the right organisation to form in life, the right career to seek, the organisation to join and even the right choice in relationships.

The secret of success is for one to find their personal assignment and start from there. That is your birthright: "Many are the plans in a man's heart, but it is the Lord's purpose that prevails." prov 19.21

No matter how a man learns how to swim, he cannot swim like a fish. We all have our own purpose for which we were created. Until you're able to discover this, you'll continue to beat about the bush. If it is not the purpose from God it will not stand. One can start anything they like, but it is God who will allow it to stand.

My people are destroyed for lack of knowledge. Hosea 4:6

Read this story:

One day, a friend asked me, to join him in a PR meeting. I was a bit hesitant, but thought otherwise since I was writing a book. I needed a fresh idea, and an environment that enhances my imagination. The client was a 70 years old woman. She looked very strong, elegant and positive. She was a manufacturer of a bespoke health product, for curing arthritis. Her story is this: she's been branding her product for 30 yrs. Her products were excellent, but her brand hasn't been able to take off. She has done advertisements, consulted different professionals and a lot of work was on ground. Yet, the brand seemed like nothing has been done.

One thing I cherished in her was her passion and commitment. Her passion for the product was hinged on the belief that she wanted to give something back to the society. She talked about her inspiration and how she discover her formulations. She went further to demonstrate how the products work and why they are different from other products in the market. The most important part of the story is this: She said, "I'm convinced you are the person that brings me the result I want. I researched about you. Your work and my spirit says to me 'you are the one who will bring the energy that will uplift my brand.'"

Within a few weeks, my friend brought in the human touch and creativity into her brand. Her products are now sold in many shops, including on high street luxury shops. The message I'm passing on is that people are waiting for your talent, your personal assignment to be fulfilled in order to receive the energy they need to uplift and drive their brands. Imagine if my friend hadn't used his talent and creativity; the woman would have been in limbo. Perhaps she would not have actualised her vision of having one of the best brands in her lifetime. This is why you don't have options but to carry out your personal assignment and purpose in life. Your generation needs what you have. If we disconnect from what really matters we end up feeling unhappy and empty. If you are not able to embark on your purpose and vision because of what people, friends and relatives will say, I bet you, you're taking more risk . People who do not go for their dreams end up with regret, especially when you see the looming danger awaiting people for not taking the right step in the right direction.

This is the tragedy of life according to Albert Einstein: "The tragedy of life is what dies inside a man while he lives." Inside you is a purpose which you never expressed.

You are a loser says Muhammed Ali: "You don't really lose, when you fight for what you believe; you lose when you fail to fight for what you cared about."

Again, it is your purpose that will make you walk 20 miles with your enemy, nothing would have made a man to do that.

"I will walk 20 miles with my enemy if there is something to learn from him," said Leibez

Our purpose in this life is to serve others. My purpose is to serve others.

Purpose is the Key

In business purpose is the key to success. What is the purpose of the company?

What human problems do I want solve?

Having known my personal assignment or what I call personal purpose in life. I would ask myself, how can I use my knowledge of personal assignment, purpose and talent to solve this specific human problem?

Remember, a company's purpose is its intrinsic reason for its existence.

How can I align my purpose in life to that of the business I want to start? Bearing in mind that the reason for forming the company must not depart from my values and vision in life.

Value is greater than money, it is beyond product and market interest. In business there comes a time when value supercedes everything.

Surely there comes a time when counting the cost and paying price aren't things to think about any more. All that matters is value – the ultimate value of what one does. James Hilton

And this idea of solving human problems gives the company its purpose, meaning and mission.

With this, the company's vision is already generated.

Having set up the intrinsic purpose of a business, the extrinsic purpose then comes up because, in a real world, business cannot run without money. The mainstay of business is profit. Without profit, a business cannot survive. This is the lifeline for all businesses. This is where solomon says: "Money is everything."

Both intrinsic and extrinsic purpose glues the different stakeholders of the company to a common mission. The stakeholders include – communities, customers, employees, suppliers and investors.

CHOICE

The greatest wealth given to humans by God is not life, but choice. We focus on life, while we tend to forget the choices available to us. Without this choice, life itself is meaningless. The choices we make will determine where we get in life. People fail in life because of poor choices. God has given us the choice of free will as essential component of love. Whoever we are, whatever we are, what matters is our choices. Do we **Respect** our choices? Humans might as well become trees that do not have choices and do not move. I do wonder when people say they are not wealthy, they don't have enough, they cannot do anything. Bruv, I'm crippled and my hands are tied. The reason we say this is because we ignore choices and options we have available to us. Jesus illustrated what choice means when he said: "Two people are in the farm; one is taken and the other rejected." This runs both in our mind and in the physical world. Look at the story of the prodigal son. He made a poor choice of leaving his father to go outside his environment, in which he was used. He suffered poverty and penury. When he realised himself, he turned back while there was still time. This illustrates why many fail in life. We are meant to connect with our God from birth, as He is our environment. And, like a fish, we can't move away from that ocean of God's presence. God's presence is the place where we connect to the right frequency that will make us flourish or blossom in all we do. This is what I called ' internal choice.' When we are born, we are supposed to continue with the right vibration and the beats in our heart, but taking a choice that is contrary to the one given to us by God only lead to poverty and mediocrity. We are meant to hook on to the infinite power to access fully that spirit given to us by God. Wrong choices set us in a collision course with our inner self—hence, we operate like a chicken instead of an eagle in an ocean of power of the universe. If you don't make the right internal choice, then the external choices will be disastrous. Saul made the wrong internal choice and he became a disaster. He killed many people. When he realised himself, he came back to God and made a right internal choice. He became a happy and successful man.

Remember, what we don't have **respect** for we don't appropriate. In fact, it has no meaning. We're the envy of the angels; we're the envy of other creatures and a city built on hills. This is the reason Satan is on the neck of many people trying to manipulate them, preventing them from understanding. He sees and acts on these choices. Without acting on these choices, you wouldn't realise your dreams. Your life won't be meaningful because of unfulfilled aspirations.

'Choice is power! Exercising it is the energy. The fire power you need for going the next level.'

Look at yourself in the mirror. Are you exercising your choices and options in your life?

Never sell your choices or mortgage your options. Think of a situation where you have monopoly, the choices are not there, the monopolist will box you into one corner, assault you heavily with the supply of substandard products, rein on you with high prices and freak you out with threat. But, you cannot do anything because your choice has been taken away. No amount of talent, tact and footworks can liberate you from this mess.

We had the choice of starting our business in 2012 or deferring it. We went ahead and started the magazine. We know the importance of personal assignment and, most importantly, the need to engage in one's talent. This has fired us up to become who we are; to express ourselves the way we would never had done had we not taken a decision. It's amazing the power of choice!

I have two kingsmen who left for Gabon in mid 70's one is called Steve and another is Christo. After two years, both were deported due to immigration. Two weeks later, it was time for both to travel back when the immigration law had been relaxed.

Steve went back but Christo decided that he was not going back for fear of what happened earlier. Fast forward to 3 year. Steve became a millionaire and Christo, who refused to go back to Gabon, continued in his life struggle. This is power of choice. Choice in itself is the key to unlocking all kinds of hidden potentials to make things happen.

Each day we need to make good choices, especially towards our goals. But everything starts by our choice of thoughts: it's vital we choose them carefully since we are products of our thoughts. They create the reality we see around us. A friend once told me to choose my words carefully, for each is a potent seed for the accomplishment of what I wish to become. Not the least: choose our actions carefully for each is the building block to all we wish to accomplish. There is no greater asset than our power to make choices. Be wise when you make choices. We have a choice of using our talent or not using it.

Remember, the world runs on the principles of talent: the one who fails to use their talent, the little one he has will be taken away and given to the one who has most. Both personal and professional relationships depend on how we maximise our choices and options. It's crucial towards achieving our goals. If you cannot act on your choices, then you cannot be on the driver's seat to navigate your way to your vision. You need to take back your power, choice is power, choice is the greatest wealth in life never to give it up.

Remember, if you can't make a choice others will make it for you and I bet you're not gonna love it. You must assume control of your destiny.

ACTION: MAKE IT HAPPEN

One can have millions of ideas in the head, not until they have the gut and courage to unleash them into action, they amount to nothing. Action is the real thing! Action is the master key. Until one understands that every word is an action and enshrines it and it becomes a culture. This changed my life forever. We say things often; so easily in our culture without meaning it. Remember, as soon as one commits oneself, then providence moves in. Nature is asking for something very simple: just begin the work and the rest follows.

The difference between success and failure is that one makes it happen, while the other do not. It is the heart and soul of business. There's no point of reading this book if you do not intend to practice the wisdom in it. If I can borrow a line from Jesus Christ: "everyone who hears these words ... and put them into practice is like a wise man who built their house on the rock." One could know as much as Einstein but not making it happen is a complete failure. Without having **Respect** for your reason for existence, purpose in life or purpose for which you are starting a business, it is impossible to carry it out. Not putting things into action will be choosing failure above success. This is like having a lamp and putting it under the table. Whatever the goals you may have, you've got to start breaking them down so that you can fly with it. One can assess oneself to know how far one is doing in terms of meeting your goals.

On the scale of 1 to 10, you can rate yourself to know how well you are currently performing. If your rate is 9 and 10, then you are on the right track. If your rate is below 8, then you need to re-evaluate yourself to know if you've understood the meaning of assignment, purpose and vision. **That strong sense of mission**. What are your values and beliefs? I was asked this question prior to the time I started embarking on my vision. I failed straight on my face. From that moment, I learnt the importance of such feedback. Your goals are tiny parts of your mission.

This result presents us with the challenge of starting from the basics, because awareness on itself is 50% of job done. If one does not understand these fundamentals, the challenge of embarking on personal assignment will be seen as hollowed. The aim of this book is to make its readers take their purpose in life as the top priority.

Regardless of any present predicament: get the philosophy. All in all, wisdom is the ultimate goal: make it happen.

Aristotle wrote, "In practical matters, the end is not mere speculative knowledge of what is to be done, but rather the doing of it."

There's magic in getting started in whatever we are doing. Action is what makes the conceptual into real. Action is power. Like I have a million pound cheque now in my hand. How can I convert it into cash? It is left for me to create ACTION in line with what I'm doing to have the cash is in my hands. The action is the only thing that converts this conceptual amount into cash which I can touch, smell, see, taste and hear and feel its crispiness. Knowledge and intelligence are both useless without action.

Carlo Rovelli, the author of a book, 'Seven Brief Lessons on Physics:'

"Heisenberg imagined that electrons do not always exist. They only exist when someone or something watches, or better, when they are interacting with something else they materialize in a place, with a calculable proba-bility, when colliding with something else. The "quantum leaps" from one orbit to another are the only means they have of being "real": an electron is a set of jumps from one interaction to another. When nothing disturbs it, it is not in any precise place. It is not in a "place" at all."

This can illustrate that without action you don't get result. It is the action that brings things into existence.

AWARENESS

Birds born in a cage think flying is an illness. **Alejandro Jodorowsky**

Concise Oxford Dictionary defines awareness as: 'conscious, not ignorant, having knowledge.' Having knowledge of something through alertness in observing, or capacity to interpreting what one sees, hears, and feels – having insight. For instance. I was reading a book titled: **'Personal Impact,' by Michael Shea.** I came across this quote: *"We're all born equal, but quite a few of us got over it by working up our image."* This instantly created a groove in my mind. This changed my perception forever and when Faustina came up with the idea for us to have C. Hub magazine, we bought into each other's passion.

Hosea: *My people perish for lack of knowledge.*

Knowledge is still power today and tomorrow. Awareness includes: Clarity, concentration and focused attention. Awareness is 50 percent the battle. Concentration helps you to focus your attention on one thing or another and this controls, regulates and commands what goes into your mind. Clarity helps to bring that mindfulness which is the presence of, the state of awareness. That ability to discern difference in two things like apple and orange, male and female, Peter and Paul. How sensitive are you picking background information, body languages? Look at the eagle that has the ability to see a tiny coin on the ground from a height of 15,000 to 20,000 ft, while a butterfly can perceive a smell about 2 to 10km away. Awareness can be raised to a reasonable level that an individual cannot forget to know that, God is watching us or that our mission is written everywhere. **Anything that is not for others is meaningless. All we do originates from and revolves around this law: 'Love thy neighbour.' This is why RESPECT is at the heart of all we do.**

For instance, energy is flowing from every thought and feeling that goes out from our mind. Look at amplifiers and lenses. They raise sounds and magnify object to a reasonable level that we hear and see from a distance. The books and magazines we read help to raise awareness so that we know what is happening around us. **The Big 'R' Of A successful Business'** brings in with it a huge awareness so that you can start your own business without breaking the bank or having a specialist idea. You don't need experience in the area of your passion, outside the one you have already. Then comes my question. Why have you not started? Why do you wait? You do not need money! You don't need that experience! So read on to know more about your mind, how to build up self – reliance, self-belief, self-confidence, self – awareness and how you can achieve your full potentials necessary to carry to an end your vision. One conquering themselves is the ultimate challenge.

And the ultimate purpose is to seek wisdom and understanding. Be aware that "If there is the shadow of a doubt on something being good for business but not truly professional, never, never, never do it. This is what brought Arthur-Andersen and Enron down.

IMAGE

The most important and the first thing God gave MAN is His image – aura, presence of God. This kind of environment gives us our perception that serve to influence things which happens around us. It's an image of perfection and sense of possibility. If you read the background of this book, then you will be able to make out for yourself what image is. Look into the mirror! What do you see? The reflection, I guess. That is how humans are the reflection of God. If you have not seen God before, have a good look into the face of your neighbour and tell me what you see. That is God you are seeing. This is what gives us self-esteem. Your self-image determines how you see the world.

Moses said that we are created in the image of God. "*Image is what gives us strong sense of mission."*

Now tell me why you will not RESPECT the image you have, the image of yourself, your family, your race, humanity, your business and your brand. Tell me why?

What image are you seeing? What is your belief? What is your perception? The image, belief, values and perception you have for one reflects the respect you have for them. This IMAGE is the most important thing that differentiates us from animals. This is where our dignity and Respect come from. *If anyone, by any means, devalues your image and you accept that—then you've been bitten and bruised so badly that all you do is fickle. You will only be teetering on the brink and in the end run into the sand. Your confidence will fizzle out leaving you empty. RESPECT comes from the image, the value one has for oneself or people. The image one holds for another attracts* **RESPECT.**

All men are born equal, but few managed to worked up their image. Do not accept any form of negative image. It is important one gives themselves a positive image. The image one gives to themselves is what others will follow.

The value of your products and services in the market depends on the image you create around them. Everything is wrapped up in the image.

From self-esteem, self-worth, self-confidence to integrity, authenticity,and originality. This is the root of all respect. This is where your identity comes from. The image is the icon that guides one throughout their journey as they go about accomplishing their mission. Strong brands do not play with their image. From their logo to identity, they think seriously before they make choices—even their brand ambassadors. Think of the picture that plays up in people's mind when the name of a brand is mentioned. What sort of signal does that sends. Is it positive or negative? Does it resonate with your customers and your audience? This plays a major role in marketing and sales. The image is about authenticity the truth in your service. What kind of confidence do people have in your product and services? Do they believe you have the capability to deliver what you said you can do? What is the probability or the odd that you can meet challenges as to deliver on time and at the location you said you will deliver? Does your product meet the standards and qualities stated? Have a look at what happened in the shares of Volkswagen products when they were caught fiddling with the pollution control. This illustrates how poor image could affect the shares and value of products in the market. What people buy is the reason for the existence – 'The Why,' cause and belief. People don't simply buy a product. It is the reason behind the product that connects with the customers. This is where loyalty comes from. Without this 'why,' the product becomes a commodity.

VISION

Where there is no vision people perish. **Proverbs 29:18**

What is it that is really important to your? Build your life around it. For whatsoever your mind circulates becomes yours. I built my life around my vision. Vision is destiny in photographs.

"Vision is the greatest gift of God to man", Dr Myles Munroe. It provides us with leadership, goals, aims, values, beliefs, motivation, and inspiration crucial for making it happen. Vision is always about the improvement of humanity. It is about the improving other people's lives. Throughout history, making a difference in the lives of others is the most crucial and meaning-ful aspects of humans. Anything that is not for others is meaningless. All originates from and revolves around this law: **'Love thy neighbour.'** This is why **RESPECT** is at the heart of all we do. Your vision is your destination. There are two most important things you need in a journey: Purpose and Destination. Without understanding, vision cannot be actualised.

Vision gives you a sense of mission which in turn gives you purpose. Vision is that unique project in your heart given to you by your creator. For the purpose of this book, it is that project you want to accomplish. It might even be your product. When a vision is accomplished, one's mission is completed and purpose achieved.

Everything follows from vision.

DR Joseph Folkman said in the book 'Drivers' written by Glenn Price & Terry Reynolds.

"I grew up in a small town in the Western United States, in the state of Utah—called Logan. To make extra money and to keep me out of trouble, my mother got me a job working for my Uncle Chester. He lived in a smaller town called Providence. My uncle was a farmer. I vividly remember a clear spring day when my uncle asked me to jump in the truck. He drove to the field on the outskirts of town where he grew wheat. At the end of the field, I spotted his yellow Caterpillar tractor parked and hooked to a plow. My uncle turn to me and announced. "You're going to plow." I was 12 years old; I had driven his other tractor once or twice before but the Caterpillar looked bigger and more powerful. All I could think of was, "Cool, this is going to be fun!"

My uncle was an excellent teacher. He sat down in the tractor seat while I stood behind him and looked over his shoulder. He explained how to start the Caterpillar tractor because the process was a bit different with a diesel. He showed me how to turn the tractor because it did not have a steering wheel, rather two levers that controlled each track and he taught me the basics of how to plow back down. When we got back to where we started, he stopped the tractor and announced, "Now it's your turn." I got in the seat and, right before I was ready to move forward my uncle said, "The most important thing about plowing is to plow straight and stay about two inches from the furrow on the left track. I confidently announced, "No problem." and started moving forward. In order to stay two inches away from the furrow, I leaned over to the left side of the tractor and watched the tract, constantly adjusting the distance between the furrow and the track. When I got to the end of the field my uncle said, "Now, look back and see how you have been doing." What I saw was a wavy furrow not a straight line. My efforts to try and keep the tractor two inches from the furrow caused me to constantly adjust the tractor to the right and then to the left. After I turned and stopped the tractor, my uncle Chester said, "I am going to teach you a principle about how to plow straight." He said, "Look down at the end of the field. Do you see that fence post straight in front of us?" I looked down the field and saw the post. He then said, "Aim for the fence post!" It turns out that when you "Aim for the fence post" you can plow straight."

From this story, You can see the young man was doing the right thing, but in a wrong way. You can't achieve your mission without aiming at your vision or your target. Your vision is your aim, target and destination. Without vision my people perish. Without vision, you cannot know where you are going. Without a vision, you are like an aircraft that has lost contact with the control centre. All successful businesses have a vision, which should be communicated to not only the management staff but to other employees during and after induction. Vision is a powerful commandment from God. Without the principle of vision, you can't do anything successful. When you understand vision, then to form habit becomes easy. Your vision will delight you. You reflect and meditate on it everyday. Aristotle says: "We are what we do repeatedly."

Look at what psalmist said: "He shall be like a tree planted by the rivers of water, that brings forth its fruit in its season, whose leaf also shall not wither and whatever he does shall prosper."

All legitimate visions are built on God. God is the foundation. You must build your vision on a solid rock that when flood and storm come, for it will not be swept away. Your vision is the most important thing in your life. Your vision is your food.

> **If you don't know where you are going, you will probably end up somewhere else. Dr Laurence J . Peter**

For one to accomplish one's vision, one must have to reclaim his mind. Some do capture their vision as early as 6 years, while it takes others more than 40 years to do the same. I captured mine when I was 8 years old, but it took me more than 40 years to rediscover myself in other for me to accomplish it. Without first reclaiming your mind, you cannot give it meaning. That sense of commitment will be absent. I saw my vision I was unable to discern it. I had no clue, but I kept on trying different things: I studied Food science to OND level, abandoned that one to study Chemical Engineering at FUTO in Nigeria. Came to England did Postgraduate Dip in Legal Studies. But when I got married, I was led to my very vision which was not clear to me. Sometimes you can be led to your calling or vision by another who you never expected. This is why **Respect** is important. *'We are a person through another person'*. One thing important about it is, whether one is prepared to accept and believe it when the moment comes, or is one gonna dwell in self-doubt and cynicism which renders that moment impotent, in carrying out your vision people will criticize you:

They will criticise you if you succeed.

They will criticise you if you fail.

They will criticise you if you speak up.

They will criticise you if you give up.

They will criticise you for being you.

They will criticise you if they think you are trying to be someone else.

No matter what, you're going to be criticised.

So, live your dream. Your vision is non-negotiable.

When you understand your vision, it gives you authenticity. It give you control over what you done. You aim over getting the best business results without neglecting both means and end. To some people 'the end justifies the means.' With legitimate vision, you will not fall into this trap.

For I know the plan I have for you; declares the Lord," "plan to prosper you and not harm you, plans to give you hope and future. **Jeremiah 29:11**

PASSION

What is unique about an individual is nothing but their passion. What is your passion?

"Passions spin the plot; We are betrayed by what is false within." **George Meredith**

Dr. Myles Munroe explained passion in a way that I've never heard nor seen another preacher done before:

"Passion is a desire that is stronger than death. It is the energy created by a purpose and meaning for life. People who have passion are willing to die for what they believe. Passion is a commitment that is beyond contention – anything that comes against you cannot stop your motivation to accomplish your dream. Passion is a thing that says to life, "I'm gonna finish you." If you can stop whatever you are doing and still be happy, you don't have passion. Passion is like something you're obligated to do. No one can stop you."

Passion is like the fuel that keeps the engine heated. When it comes to passion for your work it is non-negotiable. We have to discover something that makes us have a reason for living beyond death. When you have passion for what you are doing, then people will have to remind you to eat.

You cannot even easily get up from your bed in the morning without passion. Passion is that which fires you up. But before you have passion, you must have **Respect** for the purpose of that passion. Passion without that **Respect** is incomplete. Passion is stronger than food. Fear does not exist again because you know you have to deliver. Passion and purpose are so critical for realizing your dream.

The way one feels about what they do is important. We are humans with feelings and emotions. If you do not feel good about something, then you may not have a need for it. Good feelings can spur one to be creative and innovative.

The more passionate you are, the more you believe you have already succeeded. When you are passionate, your focus is on the goal not ego. You're focused on your destination not the journey. You do not see constructive criticisms as threats.

It's said result comes from our thought, and from our feelings come our actions and from action comes result.

A passion for the job provides energy and focus. Passion is the willingness to do whatever it takes for one to achieve their goal. Passion is the drive that makes you see 'no' as yes in other to work around it to achieve a positive result.

One can understand what Jesus said in the Bible: *"Ask, you shall be given; seek you shall find, knock it shall be opened."* Some of the wisdom is in form of instructions. If you don't follow them, then the door will not open; nothing happens, even if you pray till thy Kingdom come. Some of them you really have to ask boldly and persistently. While some of them you have to seek because they are hidden a million miles away or hidden as close inside of you. You can't go further without passion. This is what Steve Jobs said: **#1 Rule Of Success**

"People say you have to have a lot of passion for what you are doing. It is total truth because is so hard, if you don't, any rational person will give up. It is really hard and you've to do it over a sustained period of time, so if you don't love it and don't have fund and you don't really love it, you gonna give it up. And that is what happens to most people. If you really have to look at the ones successful, in the eyes of the society and the one who did succeed often time the one who succeed love what they do, so they can persevere, when it goes really tough and one did not love it, you will quit, who would want to put up with stuff if you don't love it. It is a lot of hard work and a lot of worrying constantly and if you don't love it you gonna fail. So you've got to love and you've got to have passion."

Once you discover your passion, you become a prisoner of your own success. This brings an unshakeable belief in yourself. Peter and Paul, once discovered their passion and fear disappeared. They were able to preach, regardless of any death threats. My dad, as a transporter, drove for several years and never feared death. He had passion for his work. Like I said, if you discover your personal assignment, you should never turn back regardless of any obstacle or hindrance. With this self-belief you are going to be successful. Passion is the key.

This is passion to excel, challenge and inspire.

MEANING

Meaning is how we think about our purpose, goal, aims and vision. When you have a purpose, choose a meaning that makes sense of that purpose. This will affect the meaning that you allow others to have over your purpose.

***These people honour me with their lips, but their hearts are far from me. They worship me in vain; their teachings are but rules taught by men.* Isaiah**

The meaning that we attach to our words, promise, goals, purpose, mission, vision. This is what makes it achievable. The meaning that we give to our dreams elevates them to God. Nothing changes if you don't give meaning to it. When one gives meaning to words, the divine providence listens because this is the language He understands. There is a bond between you and the words you have defined. The greatest commandment is to love neighbour; all we do hinges on that.

One of those days, I said to my wife, "I love you." She laughed, looking at me straight into the eyes she asked, "Do you really mean it?"

When we say we want to start a business, providence will instantly flash its light into our mind and ask us, "Do you really mean it?" This question is loaded.

The question must always play out in your mind. More than 95% of humans do not engage their mind in this meaning. This prompted Isaiah to say what he said. "They worship me in vain."

In all our pomp and splendour, many tend to give lip service to what we believe.

"If you're not ready to loose all you have for what you believe, you cannot achieve your vision". Muhammad Ali was striped of all his accolades for what he believed in.

Unfortunately, the world has taught many to pay lip service to their purpose and vision. This is the origin of all human failure. When your heart is far from what you're doing you cannot make good success.

Success in business is not different. The meaning you give to your business is what gets you to the height you want go. *I feel very perplexed that more than 95% people would say that they believed in something and they do not get to the end of it. This is the crisis humans face every day. Great Apostle Paul believed in the gospel he got to the end of it.*

Everything means nothing until we give meaning to them. Love does not mean anything until we give meaning to it. Beliefs have no meaning until you give meaning to them."I believe I will succeed in my business." With my heart of hearts, I believe this. Certainly you are already successful because you always get what you believe; providence and the universe will support you.

Remember, the master Jesus Christ said whatever you ask in my name you will surely have. When you give meaning to these words, they go into your subconscious. They expand because you focused on them. Why wouldn't someone **RESPECT** that which they have given meaning to? Every word has action. The meaning you give to people in life makes a great difference. In this digital era, there's a need for business leaders to adapt and be flexible to meet the needs of customers and employees. Giving meaning involves treating your staff as insiders rather than outsiders. Leadership in this era is about relationship, without this shift in paradigm, businesses will not be beneficial to the society. There wouldn't be that authenticity and there wouldn't be meaning.

FAITH / ABRAHAM

I call faith, Abraham, the father of all nations. As the name implies, faith is the father of all success. Faith will lock you in into the guiding principle of all things. God has handed to humans the most powerful tool in the universe. The tool is the word of God. Word of God was used in creating the universe. Yet, humans are afraid. Why not call in the artillery? Why not call in The Word Of God? All things work on the principle of increase and multiply. Without faith, you can't access it. Remember, all things have energy. All things have purpose and all things have one source: GOD. All things are created by God. *Faith without work is dead!* If you understand how things work, then you will know why a man that invests £1 in a business reaps £20b in 10 – 20 years time. Without first having Abraham, they will not accomplish it. All successful people in every area of their gift had Abraham. This explains why you can become successful, regardless of your family background. A street sweeper can become a millionaire from his work if he maximises the smallness. One can aspire to achieving the best results with minimum resources. A bread seller in Nigeria recently became a sensation as one of the most talked about on social media globally. If you don't have faith, then how can you maximise smallness in order to see greatness. If you have faith, there is nothing you can't achieve. Impossibility becomes possible. God is in us. Without faith, there is little or nothing you can accomplish. Abraham became a friend of God and father of nations through faith. With grain of faith, you can make things happen. God has made you God. And God lives inside you.

Faith is the expression of gratitude for man's relationship to his creator. Everything ever created by man was done against odds. Nothing great is achieved without faith. We started our business with faith that we will be able to have cash flow required to see us through. It is your faith that makes you who you are. Faith is what heals you and makes you great. More than 99% of what happens around us we don't see with our naked eyes. So, without faith, one is lost in the maze of things.

"For, Yet a little while, and the coming one will come and will not delay; but my righteous one shall live by faith, and if he shrinks back, my soul has no pleasure in him." **Hebrew 10:37**

This is one of the most powerful verses in the Bible. The way we worship God is the same way we become successful. If one has faith and persists, success will come and one's vision will be accomplished shortly. But if one wavers, dithers or shrinks, disappointment, frustration and confusion will follow them. Faith is to the world what boat is to the ocean.

PREPARATION

Ready, aim, fire.

Preparation is the evidence of faith.

Blessed is the servant, whose master comes and finds him prepared.

From birth we're supposed to be prepared all the time, honing our talent waiting for the day of opportunity. A day unique and fitted for our talent as Churchill rightly said:

"To each there comes in their lifetime a special moment when they are figuratively tapped on the shoulder and offered the chance to do a very special thing, unique to them and fitted to their talents. What a tragedy if that moment finds them unprepared or unqualified for that which could have been their finest hour."

That day is the most exciting and fulfilling in our lives. Perfect timing. But, if one is not ready, then the opportunity comes and passes.

Colin Powell once said: "Success is about preparation, hard work and learning from our failures."

Preparation means being ready—ready for a purpose, to carry out your purpose, and your personal assignment. Preparation without a purpose is meaningless. It's like life without self-examination. Preparation has to have aim, and ready for delivery. A woman conceives, grows and nurtures. She is happily expectant of the day of delivery.

Like I said, vision is vital. Humans have the ability to see the end of a project before they start the project. This is for people who have insight. Look at the architects before they design and build, they see the picture before they start building the house. This is why you see some people at age 5 and 6 years have started preparing themselves to become great with their talent by, miming, acting out in front of the mirror because they've seen their vision. Hence, they start to prepare for that finest time to manifest their talent.

Change,Time and Hard Work have no meaning if we aren't prepared to take advantage of them. One of mottos I like most is that of red cross: 'be prepared.' Hard work is useless if it is not aimed at something you are hoping to achieve. One can work as much as they like, but if they don't have purpose for it. Like the story of skirting above, the changing is going as well as time. The lady missed it at first, however, because she was not ready—despite the fact that she had the time and rope was in constant motion. Your level of confidence increases as you become well prepared. Preparation helps you put fear in a cage. When you are not prepared, it is like the lion is on the loose. To develop more confidence in what you do you also prepare yourself enough.

According to the great master, Jesus Christ, life is about preparation. If one is not prepared when the opportunity comes they miss it. Time and change is for the people who in themselves are prepared for it. Life favours people who are prepared and are at the right place and at the right time. God will uplift them. Life is about preparation waiting for that golden opportunity. If you're not focused, that much awaited opportunity may elude you. This is a tragedy. Your eyes must be fixed on the goal. Each day is a day of preparation! Even when you've got the job or position you can't afford to be complacent.

PLAN

To man belongs the plan of the heart, but from the
Lord comes the reply of the tongue. **Proverb 16:1**

In your heart you make the plan, but how you will achieve them, God will provide them to you. God will determine the steps. As soon as we decided that we want to publish C.Hub Magazine, we set our plans, by the time you know it God has provided ways to get finance and experience required to accomplish it. To some they call it the universe; the secret of success is planning.

"If you fail to plan, you've planned to fail," according to Churchill. You must have plans to achieve your goals. For instance, how and who are you going to approach for funding, whether bank or individuals, or your assets. How this will work out, is only the LORD's task, not your task any longer. Your task is to put the details or plan on the paper. "Planning is command of God", said Dr Myles Munroe. It is up to you to put your plan on paper, but how God will do it is not your business. God will direct your steps if you have a plan, but if you do not have a plan then there 's nothing for God to direct. This is how crucial it is to have a plan. As soon as you have a plan, and moving towards a goal, you're up and running. If it is skill. Know we can learn anything as long as it is relevant to what we want to do. Look at actors they identify the mannerisms, demeanour, behaviour of the role they have chosen and adopt that persona.

> *Planning is bringing the future into the present so that*
> *you can do something about it now.* **Alan Lakein**

With plans you can predict the future. Planning is a means of creating our future. And you must RESPECT your plan. Doing something is like sowing a seed. Once you got all parameters right proceed. Don't worry about what you are physically seeing. Look at when you sow seed, 'do you know how the seed sprouts out?' When you look at it critically, you may faint, yet the seed germinates. The same way is one's plan. The same way in all we do in life. Once you set your target, the universe will do the rest. All you require is the 'will'.

BELIEF

> *To them that believe, to them He has given power to be God's children.*

Beliefs are so important that they determine where we can go and what one can achieve. It defines how we see the world and act within it. Beliefs are ideas we think are true. Our beliefs come from our physical environments;

Parents, friends, relatives, teachers, religion, our experiences in life all in all from our culture. Unless one moves away from these environments that have suckered us to believe that we cannot shape our future and live a fulfilled life of happiness, joy and love, then we cannot achieve our full potentials. We do have in our minds limiting beliefs and they are negative ideas we have concerning our identity,capabilities, other people and the world. Limiting beliefs affect our psyche, control how we interpret our experience and stifle our abilities and finally prevent us from achieving our goals in lives. The limiting beliefs function like a conditioning in our mind, for me they are responsible for poverty in the world where we have abundant resources.

These beliefs are what disempower, imprison and cripple people and make many paupers and blind. Hosea, in his word, said that these people are destroyed for lack of knowledge. Knowledge that is understood and applied is power. Knowing something is different from believing it to be true. You must move away from wrong beliefs and take responsibility of your actions. We need to be clever here. If you fail to understand this fact, then you are ruined and kept in bondage. All successful men and women moved away from this culture of ignorance to a culture of wisdom, love and power. If you believe you can start your business and become the best in your area of operation, you'll have it achieved. No one can stop you from achieving what you planned because it has been given to you by God before the creation of the world. The only person that can stop you is you because you have opened your mind to wrong belief system that is wrongly rooted on myths. It is your choice to go along with such myths and assumptions that stop you from starting the business, that career, relationship that aspiration . Don't close your mind to this powerful gift from God. Knowledge is objective but belief is subjective.

Believe in yourself and everything becomes possible. Be proud of who you are. If you don't believe in yourself then there is nothing you can do. Believing in yourself means having confidence in yourself. When you believe in yourself, it means you can always do what it takes. That you will ultimately arrive at your destination. This a critical point. Like an aircraft, you are on a point of no return. Remember Mrs. Margaret Thatcher once said: "I've no reverse gear," You are Northbound, You've engaged the lifting gear, it is too late to go back. In fact going back is impossible. Friends and family members would say: 'You did not tell us that you want to start business, oh we would have helped you the more. Tell them that they can help you now.

A friend once told me " Emeka, I've been here all the while with you, but you didn't tell me you wanted to start Magazine business. Do you know that I've worked in a magazine business before? I would have helped you. I told him, "It just happened, bro. Don't fall prey to many and various forms of sympathies that are in disguise to torpedo your dreams thereby making you your worst enemy. Remember, you have different personality with these people, do not allow them to control your thoughts and actions. YOU'VE BEEN REVEALED TO YOURSELF.

If I can borrow a line from Jesus: "No one who holds a plough and looks back is worth a salt." If one does not believe they can achieve something, then how can they achieve it? Once you have strong belief that you can make it, you will make. The problem is self-doubt, wavering, fear. Dr Myles said fear is evidence of ignorance. Another one says fear is an acknowledgement of influence of evil and connotes a lack of belief in their creator. This book **'The Big 'R' Of A Successful Business'**, was not what I intended doing when I met Mr. Reddy. My intention was to write an article to put on our website and the title of the article was, **'How to succeed in business.'** But, to my utter amazement, not only was Mr. Reddy able to give me the 3 things required in business but also sparked up a fire to start writing the book. Though I was prepared in mind to write the book and when that moment called, "I believed it" there was no doubt or any contemplation whether to do it or not. That time was the 'Eureka' moment.

A belief in oneself gives one confidence to step into the unknown and persuade others to go where one has never gone before. One might entertain a belief that life is easy; therefore, you don't need to work hard. When you encounter tasks that are hard, they might start feeling sick. They go into the procrastination bin at the end. Your belief changes the way you pursue your vision, goal, mission and purpose. The gap between where you are now and where you intend to be is belief. God has probably shown you your vision, or you have a vision of what you want to achieve in career, relationship and in business. You feel you are not yet there. What is delaying it? Is it simply that you have not strengthened your belief? You got to believe it before you can have it. You got to have your vision in your memory and replay it all the time. You are the first person who must believe in your vision before any other person. If you don't believe in it, then how can any other person believe in it?

'If you are weak, you say I'm strong
If you are poor, you say, I'm rich.

Whatever we believe and confess you have.'

Anything that is not for others is meaningless. All we do originates from and revolves around this law: 'Love thy neighbour.' This is why RESPECT is at heart of all we do.

TALENT IS GOLD

Where the needs of the world and your talents cross, there lies your vocation. **Aristotle**

The world is run on the principle of talent. You run the world with your talent. Anyone who fails to use their talent, even the one they have, will be taken away and be given to one who has more. Your success in life depends on your ability to maximise your talent. This is new era. Anyone without talent won't be able to compete in the world. We have more than 7 billion people in the world. If one fails to identify their talent; I'm afraid they would find it extreme difficult to have influence in the world.

Talent is that vital thing one does: What is in your hand passionately and effortlessly at all times in all situations without which you are not who you are? We are children of God. You find greatness when you maximise smallness.

One of the most powerful speakers of the 60s once asked his audience, "what is it in your hand?" Talent is the work in our hands; that ability to transform ideas into action. Our hands and brain are the evidence to demonstrate that God has given us the ultimate power to create just like Him. Talent is the work we love to do everyday effortlessly and naturally. There is a song, "Doing what comes naturally." This is one of the greatest gifts God endowed us with. It is the area of our leadership and our influence. With your talent, you can achieve your purpose and vision. It's your talent that drives happiness, personality and aspiration.

Talent is what made Usain Bolt, Pele, Muhammad Ali, Bill Gate, Steve Job and Nelson Mandela achieve their visions. Understanding oneself begins when we discover our talent. Your talent is your own DNA. Talent is the language one uses to relate to themselves and others. This is where you express yourself, your independence, authority, authenticity,originality, character, identity and freedom. For me, it's an expression of oneself. According Balotelli, "football is a way of expressing my freedom."

This is the area of our victory, success, and dominion. This is where everyone is made complete and lack nothing. This is an area our background, criticism, hatred and or environment cannot stop us from soaring to the top. The problem is being able to identify your talent. That has been a problem for many since the beginning of time.

We need to first define the problem. If I had an hour to save the world, I would spend 59 minutes defining the problem and one minute finding solutions. **Albert Einstein**

The problem everyone faces is identifying their talent and once you're able to do that, your problem in the world is solved. In fact, if one knows their talent and locks into that frequency, then they are unstoppable. The great scientist Albert Einstein also noted that: "Once I'm locked into what I love to do, the only thing that will stop me is putting a bullet on my head." What connects you to the universe is your talent; never play with it. It is priceless.

Jesse Owen one of the greatest athletes of all times, in 1936 subverted huge prejudice both at home and Berlin to become the world champion. He won 100 meters, 200 meters 4x100 relay and long jump.

There was once a preacher who was going about asking people their problems. As he moved, he has one question he was asking his followers. "What is your problem?" As soon you mention your problem, let say "money," he would give you money. Next, he moves to another person and he says: "What is your problem, lady?" The lady says, "Car." And, he gives her a car. Next, he moved to another person. The next person said, "hand pain." He healed him. One would then ask, "How was he able to solve people's problems? As everyone was having a different problem, he was going about revealing each person his own talent.

Your talent is your power and you must engage it into work. We need to recognise the importance and have RESPECT for it. Your talent gives one their area of influence and dominion. To be highly successful you have to work more on yourself than you work on your job as John Rohn said. If an axe is sharpened, more work is done. The most important place to invest is on your talent, and it must start with your mind.

In President Nelson Mandela's inaugural Speech he said;

"We ask ourselves: Who am I to be brilliant, gorgeous, talented, fabulous? Actually, who are you not to be?

You are a child of God.

Your playing small doesn't serve the world.

There's nothing enlightening about shrinking so that other people around you won't feel insecure.

We are all meant to shine as children do.

We are born to manifest the glory of God that is within us. It is not just in some of us; it is in everyone.

And as we let our light shine, we unconsciously give other people permission to do the same. As we are liberated from our own fear, our presence automatically releases others."

Your Talent is where your power is but, the biggest challenge to your talent is your mindset towards the giver. What is your mindset towards God? Do you have a negative mindset towards God like the one given one talent in the Bible? The mindset of doubt, depression and negativity? Have you forgotten that if you are complaining, the law of attraction will reflect back those thoughts to you? When the Master called for him to give account, what he got was punishment. It attracted all of which he was complaining. I just hope you don't have that mindset towards a giver. You need to hone your talent everyday in preparation and anticipation for great opportunities.

St Paul said, "Transform yourself by the daily renewal of your mind." We need to hone our talent daily preparing for the day of opportunity, a special day, unique and fitted for our talent. Your talent leads you to a place flowing with milk and honey. There is no need to ask a fish to climb a tree said Albert Einstein. Your talent is for you to personally actualise your assignment, purpose, vision and mission.

You're God's powerhouse. Go light the world in your own wonderful way. Your talent is essential if you want to have an enduring happiness and joy. Do not allow what people, friends and relatives would say prevent you from honing your talent or to go for your vision, if you do, then you are taking more risks. Your talent is your gift. Many people spend 20, 30, 40, 50, 60, 70, 80, 90, and 100 years and will never opened their gift. This is the greatest tragedy. An unopened gift is a tragedy. You must access your talent and quickly trade with it.

Distinction is our power. If you are not different, then what use are you? Your talent is what distinguishes you from the pack. A product is important because of its uniqueness. So are humans. Without your talent, you are not important as another person can replace you. God gave each person different fingerprints; our talent is just as unique. Talent is like buds —they are nurtured and nourished until their petals slowly open and prepare for the very nature in life. Rain falls and sun shines. They grow and grow till they become big flowers shining and attracting people. Talent is nurtured and nourished through constant practice. They go through a test. Under rain and sun It sweats and fires before they form what is called gold. Until one perfects their talent, they would not solve the needs of the world. This makes it necessary that one has to go through the required rigor to achieve the best result. So, identify your talent, hone it with knowledge and skills and you are already hitting the ground running. Do not forget that there's a saying: "Hard Work beats talent when talent fail to work hard."

FEAR

"For God hath not given us the spirit of fear; but of power,
and of love, and of a sound mind." 2 Tim1:7

Love, power and wisdom is what God has given to us. These three components are the building blocks you can use to construct or design anything you want. But as soon as you include fear into it, that's the end because you have introduced the devil in your project. You have introduced 'Project Fear.' You cannot possibly do anymore. You can't possibly start your own business, nor can you engage in any good relationship. Your career and aspirations run into sands leaving you only with self pity, self doubt and mistrust.

Ronald Reagan said; "Evil is powerless if the good are unafraid."

The breath that God gave us is His own Spirit. He breathed into man – male and female the same spirit. Why would men discriminate against women, and why would people discriminate against others since they have the same spirit of God? Discrimination is the evidence of fear, and fear is the evidence of presence of the devil. In the spirit world, there is no male and there is female. Why can't we allow the will of God to happen on earth? In front of God, all are equal—including children.

"Fear is the evidence of ignorance," according Dr. Myles Munroe. Fear is the acknowledgement of the influence of the evil. It connotes lack of belief in one's creator.

Fear is the root cause of insecurity, anxiety, extremism, racism, hatred and anger. It creates a fixed mindset that makes many people not to learn or accept positive changes. Many politicians know of this and they exploit the 'project fear' to manipulate and control the masses since many live in fear already. Unless one sees fear in a broader context, one would know that fear comes from the devil.

We cannot build on our weaknesses: fear, anger and hatred. When we build on fear, it becomes difficult to contemplate a bold and positive action and bring it to life. Translating words into action is the ultimate goal. Not making things happen is to build on fear. With fear, you cannot have a leg to stand on—let alone, starting a business. Fear makes you not to have self-confidence.

Fear is a virus that wrecks everything that makes you human.

They say fear is an apparition and apparition is a mental ghost which exist only in the imagination of the perceiver.

> *"Fear destroys our critical faculty.*
> *Fear weakens our self-confidence.*
> *Fear shatters our self-esteem.*
> *Fear undermines our self-will.*
> *Fear devalues our self-worth.*
> *Fear leads us to uncertain purpose."*
> **Unknown**

What drives one is success and fear of failure. The fear here is a positive one because you don't want to fail. 'I must do this so that I don't fail.' This motivates you, therefore make you not to rest until you get a better result. This is incentive.

We have fear of success. This is dangerous. Like, 'I can't do this.' one already accept defeat before giving it a go.

Feel the fear but don't allow it to hold you back. Don't focus on what others will think of you. Just remember that people have their insecurities as well. They are also thinking of theirs and not you. Fear is the Mount Everest in your mind. The big mountain you need to level out. You must conquer it if you must achieve any great thing in your life. Fear is a malignant disease ravaging man's power over nature. Fear breeds hatred, anger, aggression, suspicion, disorderliness, insecurity and lack of self-confidence.

A good warrior will get out the trench and march towards the enemy even though he's terrified. **Marvin Gaye**

We have strong instincts which we fall back to: The Fight, Flight, Freeze (FFF) response mechanism. Your ability to choose any of these determines your outcome. Fight is taking on the threat; Flight means escaping and running away from perceived danger. Then Freeze is keeping still and somehow hoping that the danger will go away, probably not noticed. Accepting the terms and condition, blending and avoiding that problem. Certain situations need to be tackled head on. Fear can make you take to flight or freeze, because one is afraid that situation. We tend to forget that challenges don't actually exist, unless you persist you will think there is no way. Nothing can resist human mind. This fear prompts us to freeze or take to flight. Sometimes the fear makes you strong and bold. The power to overcome the natural human tendency puts us ahead. We need to train ourselves to jump and leave the edge where majority are trapped as a result of fear. Trapped in the feelings of what others may be thinking of you. In that cocoon is a cauldron of controls and limitations.

When I imagine my school days, I could still touch, see, smell, hear and feel the cauldron that imprisoned me. It held me back like a formidable force: preventing me from entering the four walls of the university, whenever I had problems. In my mind, it was a loud noise: "What will other students be thinking of me." Little did I know that people I was thinking about, were too busy with their lives and problems. The world does not care about what you are thinking, so go ahead with your vision and goal. Your experience, vision and purpose are unique, people are not aware of them.

I live for being on stage. The exchange with the audience. The rush of not knowing if you're going to fall on your face or soar to the skies is very appealing. **Unknown**

What you have to know is that God is right inside you, therefore nothing is impossible.

Consider this wisdom from 'Womenworking.com';

"'The devil whispered in my ear, "You're not strong enough to withstand the storm."

Today, I whispered in the devil's ear, "I am the storm."'"

Fear is a powerful motivating factor. For instance, the fear of not getting a required result makes me to work hard. Many things we see as negative could help us achieve positive result. Harnessing this energy is vital. "Fear too is an invitation to experience courage," according to Bill Treasurer in his book. "Courage Goes To Work." One should not allow fear to hold them back. The future always belong to the fearless. Don't fear for the worst, but be driven for the best. If we all stop pushing boundaries because of fear, then things will never change. Man will not go to space, music will not inspire people, products won't argument our capabilities. Fear will make us not to question status quo, not challenge ideas and myths that enslave humanity. Every generation has a chance to be great, how can we be great when we let fear paralyse us? Know that fear has energy. And ability to exploit this energy to achieve positive result is breathtaking.

STRATEGY

Strategy always changes the rule of the game. You cannot win or become successful if you don't have strategy.

***If the axe is dull and its edge unsharpened, more strength is needed but skill will bring success.* Ecclesiastes 10:10**

It's not just working hard, it is working skillfully and smartly. To have knowledge of law is to work smartly.

First thing first: See every challenge as an opportunity.

It's not what you say but how you say it that matters. Planning is important, but strategy is more important. Planning is like steps to achieve a goal. Strategy is how you're going to execute those steps. Strategy always changes the rules of the game. In my leadership video on YouTube, I stated the importance of strategy for a leader. First and foremost, a leader has to understand their strengths and weaknesses. One cannot beat their competitors if they fail to work on their strength. Never attack your rivals on their strength. If one does, they will be beaten hands down. By engaging your rivals on your strength, you have automatically changed the rule of the game.

For me, there was no other fight in history of boxing where strategy played a huge and exciting role than the 1976 world boxing championship held in kinshasa – Republic Of Congo. The fight was dubbed **"Rumble In The Jungle."** The bout was between Muhammad Ali and George Foreman. George was booked to win the fight because he was a power house. But in an ironic turn of history Ali upturned the stage to the surprise of the world and the pundit. Ali took Foreman by storm to become the undisputed heavyweight champion. Ali operated on his strengths here.

Even the story of the seven foolish virgins showed the power of strategy. Saving cost is a powerful strategy. Humility is a strategy. Respect is a strategy. Jesus Christ said to his disciples to be as wise as serpent and innocent as dove. You cannot be a businessman without being strategic. All wars are won and lost on the field of strategy. Battle of the mind is the battle of strategy. A man cannot kill a Lion except through strategy.

Two things are important:

1. You must be on the right track.
2. You must be moving.

You can look at strategy in this context: A friend told me a story of what happened where a big and prestigious hospital was ran down for many years. A great hospital administrator was appointed to oversee the entire hospital. He decided to bring excellence, standard and focus. He concentrated on one area: Emergency Room (RM). He made it possible for any patient that arrived to be seen by highly talented doctors and within a specified time. Mostly in minutes. After one year, he had transformed the ER and it became a model for the entire hospital. From this difference made by the administrator, this hospital became a model for other hospitals in that country. Always ask yourself how and where you achieve a positive result and use it to make a difference. It's necessary to monitor your progress. Your success requires you measure it. This will enable you to know when to change your strategies.

Business is a form of hunting. Look at lions; they lay ambush in a specific location, waiting patiently for their prey. They know the route their prey pass. They could wait for hours. They are focused, persistent, consistent and they are operating on their strengths. They don't allow their prey to detect the battle ground or to change the rule of the game. The same applies to all battles and businesses. One's success in every battle or business is largely dependant on your ability to change the rule of the game by not allowing your opponent to strategically drag one to their own area of strength. This is always a tactical and strategic error. To win, you must not allow your opponent to lure or distract from your own area of strength. When you build on your strength like lions, you are unbeatable and unstoppable. Focus on your strengths. Maximise on your strength.

If you want a different result you have to put a different thing. It is insanity to expect a different result when you keep on doing the same thing all over and all over.

You have to change your attitude to get a different result if you don't like the result you are getting.

The say the champions are people who do the same thing we do but differently. You must move your mindset from the problem to the solution. I refer you to section B, where I demonstrated how to solve problem.

ADAPTABILITY

It is not the strongest of the species that survives nor the most intelligent but the one most responsive to change. **Charles Darwin**

As I am writing this, Twitter loses four executives as it battles to attract customers. According to Metro Tuesday, Jan 26 2016 page 21.

"Twitter's stock price has 38% since Mr Dorsey returned to the microblogging site last year over concerns how the site – which has about 300 million users – can compete with rivals such as facebook, which has 1.4billion members. He has already cut the workforce by eight per cent. Twitter has also struggled to compete with the rise of Instagram and snapchat amid rumours it may follow China's Sina Weibo – a similar site – and remove its 140 – character limit."

This is how hot the market is: serious competition is going on out there. If you fail to innovate, adapt and be flexible you are out of business. God said his message is new every morning. This is an important principle that keeps all businesses relevant. It's like this: when one is in a river, you have to swim or you sink. You have to stretch and flap as you go along the business waters. When we started to publish the magazine, it was pretty difficult to keep up with pace of changes in the market: we really have to adapt and reinvent as what the customers demand and want were always changing. These challenges are what make businesses exciting as well as risky. UK alone had about 299,900 businesses at the beginning 2015, as the year winds up about 218,009 business had gone under. What is the reason? Majority of businesses do not appreciate how fast things change within one month of starting a business and they failed to plan against the rainy day especially in terms of what time they will start having return on investment. This is usually a huge trap in business. People do have that complacency of thinking that immediately I start business everything will fall into place. But it does not work like that. You've got to face challenges, even when we know they don't truly exist we can create it by our thoughts and feelings. You need to be wise, know when to be flexible and when not to be. Know when to be adaptable and when not to be adaptable. Joseph in the Bible used to grow beards. When the time came to head the Egyptians, he cut his beard to suit time and his purpose. I always ask, "Why will a man walk 20 miles with the enemy if not for their purpose in life?" Your purpose takes priority over every other thing. Hence, you got to adapt. Until companies and people understand the meaning of purpose, They will not be able to adapt.

What lady Macbeth said to her husband:

"To beguile the time, look like the time."

The successful like to respond to situations in 3 ways. Firstly, adapting in a way they fit to the environment. Secondly, Shaping the environment – contributing and having influence on the changes they want. Look at social media today was developed by change makers. People who had hunger for change in the way humans can interact.

What role are you playing to shape the nature of things going on the internet? The third is Selection. – Your ability to move to the new environment puts the future in your hands. All these lead to having control of your destiny in your hand. This leads one to taking back control of their freedom. This is the aim of adaptability.

CHALLENGES

Challenge they say is opportunity. Opportunity to excel, inspire and motivate and to be great.

All challenges are there to promote you, serve and elevate you. They bring you face to face with commitment, your values. They reveal your mindset. This only happens if you see challenges as empty threats, scare tactics from the powerless one to prevent you from realising your aims, objectives and goals in life. Challenges are there to freak you out if you are not clued up. They are there to dim your light like a fog.

In a real sense of it, a challenge does not exist because God has set us on the path of success from the beginning. From the beginning you have a prosperous future. God lives inside us. But when you face doubt and fear, you begin to attract to yourself obstacles and problems along this part of success. Great men like David knew from the start that the so-claimed challenge doesn't exist. They are mirages, like what you see on the road as you drive along a clear highway. Fear and doubt in your mind introduce this mirage. Instantly it expands and comes into existence. We have the power to bring it into existence. Good or bad things will happen, depending on our choice. Remember, 'you can speak your word into existence.' We have enormous will power given to us by God. Sadly, we abuse it.

Of course, challenges are in everything we do because we call it into existence. Remember at the beginning, death had no impact on Adam. It literally did not exist, but as soon as Adam sinned, he activated it. Even when we activate them, they are there to elevate us to the next level of success. But if you fear, you'd have given it power over yourself. One of the reasons people don't succeed is because they run away from challenges and responsibilities. If you postpone it, then it still await you.

We were faced with financial challenges when we wanted to start the magazine. Many people would have given in when faced with such an enormous obstacle, but we did not allow it to stop us. Instead, we carried on without fearing because we have faith in God that we will overcome it. Here we are, celebrating and exhilarating and thinking about the single decision we took. The decision not to quit was the best decision. Challenges lock you into the promise of increase and multiply. When David saw Goliath, it was a huge challenge for Israelites and not himself. He had understanding and wisdom. But with understanding and faith, he knew he could always win over Goliath, regardless of his long years of experience in war. That challenge was a great opportunity for him to shine and he took a chance. This single challenge changed the dynamics of things not only for him but also for the rest of his countrymen. Without stepping up and challenging certain situations one cannot lock into the principles of success. Step up and start whatever you want to embark on and you will see how successful you will become. Don't wait and don't over scrutinise yourself. *There is always no time to prepare enough, but there is always a time to do it again. Challenge tests you and introduces you to yourself.*

There was one Sunday in Lagos that a huge loud of explosive was heard all over the city. There was a state of pandemonium. Buildings were shaking, as if there was earthquake. At a hospital, many patients who had not moved their body for months, and were only fed by nurses, were in fact bedridden. On that fateful day, all of them were seen running for their lives without nurses' aid. Before that day, it appeared impossible for them to move out of bed, let alone through the hospital doors. It is our mind that breeds that impossibilities. They become a huge weight on our will power that we never move an inch. Every obstacle or challenge is opportunity and God has given that situation into your hand. You must have heard a story of two men sent off to market shoes in one continent with a prospect of setting a shoe business. One sent back a message saying: "Situation is hopeless, stop, no one wears shoes in this part of the world."

The other person sent a different message triumphantly: "Fantastic opportunity since they have no shoes; a glorious business opportunity."

Even people asked to spy in the Bible, there were twelve men, ten men came back with bad tidings while the other two came back with good tidings. The two saw that challenge as opportunity, the same applied to the shoe seller. **All obstacles, to me, are opportunities.**

COMMUNICATION

Good communications are essential if one must be successful in business. Look at organs in body. They are able to naturally coordinate because there's a form of communication within the body structure.

Communication is so vital that nothing is done in life without communication. Everything will be in paralysis without communication. Values,
beliefs, vision and ideas will never be shared with others without communication. There is no communication if there is no feedback or response.
Communication should be a two way traffic.

Remember God said: "So shall my word be that goes out from my mouth:
It shall not return to me empty, but it shall accomplish that which I purpose,
and shall succeed in the things for which I sent it." Isaiah 55:11

Communication must be made simple so that one at the end of either
channel will understand. If nothing is understood, then nothing is done.
Effective communication is vital if a business owner needs to share their
vision to their employers. If the vision is not communicated properly, then
you find that people will be working in darkness. Effective communication
creates a conducive environment for relationships to flourish. For us to have
effective communication, there must be clarity and words used should not
be ambiguous as not to create confusion to the listener. Good communica-
tors make great impact to our lives. As a leader—your ideas, thoughts, and
feelings are like seed. They only yield results if they are planted. If they are
not communicated, then they don't produce a required results. Even if you
have the best brains and good listeners, your ideas, thoughts and feeling
must be communicated before they can have impact on people. People don't
know what is in your mind. Once you have spoken, words begin to form
pictures creating ranges and breath in the mind of the listener that when
they capture them they are fixed in their brain that they might be there
forever. It is not what you said but how you said it. The tone and authority
in your voice that creates ranges and breaths that result in a huge impact.
Effective communication softens and melt down grievances, doubts, jealousy, ambiguity, mistrust and indecision. It levels ground creating a conducive
environment for good relationship between employers and employees to
flourish. With this in place good ideas, thoughts and feelings will spring
up and grow to a level they will benefit all – employers, employees and customers. Without effective communication, there is no channel linking the
employer and employees, vision and purpose will disappear best leading to
demise of the company.

Let's hear what Dr Myles says: "There is nothing more powerful like idea.
Ideas are the raw material for creation of concept. Concepts are produced by
ideas. Concept are the source of communication. They are the foundation

for our communication and it determines the success of our understanding. If you don't have the same concept as I have, then you and I cannot understand each other. You need to get the right concept from people to properly understand them." In organisation communication, it is essential in relating both strategy and vision to the whole employees. Employers cannot effectively impact the culture of the organisation if there is poor communication. There is no other better channel to inspire and motivate your workers other than effective communication. Communication includes that which was not said but can be perceived. The whole process of communication requires feedback; without feedback, there was no communication. Communication comes across in the way you express yourself, ideas, voice tone, your entire body language.

Listening is a form of communication which is the most important. I always say 95 percent of all that God-created are silent. They are silent in order to listen. This is great wisdom in listening. You listen to hear the difference in people, to hear their joy, happiness, sorrow, cry and pain. You listen to hear people's stories of triumphs and defeat. For instance, if a client works up to you, they expect you to listen attentively to know their problem before they could be solved. If you don't listen, they will be frustrated and that forms a bad impression of you. Breakdown in workplace is always attributed to poor listening. If you don't listen to people, then you will not understand them and nothing positive is achieved. Time is wasted and time is money. Effective listening promotes and helps one to understand people's thoughts, feelings and actions. Silence is a form of communication. They say still water runs deep.

> **Stillness is not just an indulgence for those with enough resources – It's a necessity for anyone. Pico Iyer**

Achieving the best results with a minimum amount of words should be what a good communicator aspires. Don't forget that every word is an action, so keep it simple. The mind controls everything one does. Communication plays a vital role in influencing one and the most fitted for the mind. It can soften or harden one depending how it's used. Often the context detects the tone and the message that is communicated. For instance, your audience determines your message and tone to use to deliver it. The tone and message you give at a women's gathering should be different from when you are talking to an audience of men or both genders.

Communication is not only about right attitude but about a careful attention to language. How do you phrase your word to empower others or give them opportunity to respond from a position of strength? We should not communicate in patronising or condescending manner to your customers and clients. Like I say, ***Respect is an act of discipline we all need to learn if we are going to be successful in business.***

CHANGE

Change is the only thing that is constant; managing it is worth investing our time.

All changes start with oneself. If you want to change the world, you must first change yourself.

Charity, they say, begins at home. The first place to begin the change is the mind because this is where the greatest battle is fought. If you can capture a person's mind, then you have transformed him. This is why they say writers rule the world. We must always be prepared for the changes coming to our shore. We should not be afraid of changes, but rather take advantage of changes to better our future by riding on the waves of changes coming our way. We, as business people, should take advantage of changes such as social media. It helps us to reinvent and rediscover ourselves, instead of impeding these positive changes. All human creations are full of imperfection, but success is learning and improving what we have. We are prepared from our mother's womb for whatever talent we may have. All we do is to hone our talent to be in line with our vision and the changes taking place on our shores. We must ride on the crest of waves and direct these waves of changes to our vision. Our destiny is in our hands. It needs courage, commitment and determination. If we know where we are going, the waves of change can always take us to our destination. There is no need to build a bulwark against changes for they are there to serve us if we know our purpose and destination.

Someone once said, "Change come disguised as an enemy only to those who refuse to see it as a friend."

Not all changes are the same. Change with anxiety does not bring in progress rather disaster. But change comes with enthusiasm. Its product is progress and this is the kind of change we are talking about.

CHANGE + ENTHUSIASM = PROGRESS

CHANGE + ANXIETY(FEAR) = DISASTER

Changes come so slowly. It's not because they are not good or lack enthusiasm, but most people who are benefitting from status quo are so fearful of what the new situation will be for them. Fear contributes immensely to this insecurity and prevents one from seeing the change that has begun to break through the gloom of the past. To assume that changes will be taken onboard is to be naive, even the best ideas need to be sold to the people. This is where the crux of the matter lies. Many will be skeptical and resistant. We know human progress always has been slow because people are reluctant to accept new ideas. Change itself is frightening to many, but you've got to remember what Le Carre said: "Frightened people never learn." Change is not event but a process. People move through 5 stages before adopting the changes or rejecting it. We have knowledge, persuasion, decision, implementation and confirmation.

Let's at SWOT (Strength, Weakness, Opportunity and Threat)

STRENGTH: Our strength is our passion and talent and that is the area we must invest in. We have to invest in personal development more than in our job to prepare for the changes coming our way. Our strength is in creating opportunities. Be wise to make more opportunities than you find. We need to focus on our strength, for we are often our own worst critic. We censor ourselves, minimising our strength and successes but maximising our weaknesses and failures. Don't allow self-chattering run negative movies or do pity party in your mind. This behaviour makes us to lose faith. God only look at our strengths, therefore we must play to our strengths. We have to keep on playing to our strength till it becomes a habit.

WEAKNESS: Our weakness is that we fail to prepare enough for the changes coming. We don't have an open mind to be receptive to the changes; we hire the wrong people and move around with the wrong people. We open up businesses that we don't have interest and passion for. We spend majority of time studying the wrong courses in the university that we find it difficult to raise our heads in the water. We fear to stand for what we believe and we fail to be comfortable in our skin.

OPPORTUNITY: See change as an opportunity and not a threat. Opportunity to do those things which we were not able to do in the past. Now is the time to do them.

Benjamin Disraeli said, "Opportunity is more powerful, even than the conquerors and prophets." Make and create more opportunities for your people. There's no love greater than creating more opportunities where people can exercise their choices and options. The greatest wealth given to man by God is not life but choices and you must act on your choices and options. This is the best way to take advantage of changes going on. Always think of opportunities to create rather than waiting for others. A wise man makes more opportunities than he finds." – Francois Bacon. And a Hindu proverb says, "A man who misses his opportunities, and a Monkey who misses his branch, cannot be saved." By creating opportunities, you're serving others and in that way you are great. You would have changed yourself and automatically changed the world. You have probably realised your dreams, joy and happiness will follow you all the days of your life because you have seen the Lord in the land of the living.

THREAT: You must know your competitors, environment, and time that militate against you. Never build a cocoon around you; it is the worst strategy. You have left yourself defenceless and started giving your opponent that vital power to throw you out of business. You must spend time to study your competitors, know their strategies and be able to read their signal. Never be complacent and take them for granted. You should always be one step ahead of them. You must continue to transform yourself, while encouraging creativity and innovations. The threat you are facing makes you take a snapshot of your competitors. With this, you can evaluate and develop a picture. Place it under a microscope, analyze what is happening and set a new trend. This opens window of opportunity that will change the course of things.

Time is a threat but, if you study it, then it can be to your advantage. You must know when to go in and when to leave. But if you do not pay attention, then it works against you.

Environment includes government regulations, law and community. You have to study them as animals study their environment to see whether they suit the business with such vision and mission. All threats can work in your favour if you pay attention to them.

How to implement change:

1. A single vision shared and preached across the board.
2. Right people to do the job to bring the change desired.
3. Tools and resources that aims at bringing the intended change.
4. Action plan to support the change.

LEADERSHIP

The most important challenge facing the world is not terrorism, hunger, nuclear atomic bomb, or poverty, it is leadership. If one makes a lion leader of the flocks of sheep, they will be highly successful. But if one makes a sheep the leader of lions, they will be defeated in all battle. This is how important leadership is in every human relationship. From the time of Adam to our time, man has been facing leadership problems. We possess the same will as God. This is His gift to man, and nothing can resist human will. So the top priority of a leader is to become himself, like the top priority of a seed is to become a tree with fruits on it. So your top priority is to become God, don't forget you are a child of God.

A leader takes complete ownership of whatever goes wrong. A leader takes responsibility of everything and accomplishes what people thought was not possible.

A leader is a person who has vision and can hear, understand and apply the loud voice of silence. Everything created by God has energy and all of them talk. Your insight as a leader is what makes a difference. Your ability to hear and understand the distinct voices gives you an edge over others. For instance, A baby can be silent, but the eyes will speak her real feelings. The stars and moons all speak out the real feelings of God and He is watching us.

Martin Luther King Jr. said: *"Everybody can be great because everybody can serve."*

First and foremost, you must see yourself as a servant and you must maximise the smallness to be great. I, for one, have never seen anyone who cannot serve. In effect, we're all leaders. Martin Luther Jr is linking greatness with service. The great Psalmist David said: "We're wonderfully and fearfully made." This, again, puts us in the forefront as leaders.

Unless you see yourself as a leader, you have little or nothing to appropriate. You are a leader in your own area of gifting. You are unique, and sophisticated with a powerful talent and brain. You are crowned with a powerful mind capable of solving any problem. This is confirmed by one of the greatest scientist, Albert Einstein; *"Everybody is a genius. But if you judge a fish by its ability to climb a tree, it will live its whole life believing it is stupid."*

Does this not stimulate you? Tell me! He is saying everybody is a success story, everybody is a leader in his area of gifting, in the area where God has given you talent. If you judge everybody, then you're doing a disservice to that person. If you judge everybody on their skills on mathematics; you make them look bad, which we are not supposed to do. Sadly, the world tends to mumble-jumble everything together and call people bad names. This is one of the tragedies of life.

Leaders love positive changes and they love to make a difference by engaging others.

Respect means finding value in what we have. We must only build on our strengths. Don't weigh or judge someone on their weaknesses.

God only judges us on our strengths, therefore you must look at people's strengths not their weaknesses. Majority of people build on weaknesses: fear, anger, hatred, envy, jealousy and prejudice.

Leaders are in love with their work, people and customers. Hence, in love they have **Respect** for themselves, people, customers and their products and services.

They believe in themselves and have sense of possibilities. They walk the walk, and lead by example. You have to believe in yourself. Believe in people and people have to believe in you. If you don't have respect for yourself, people, or your product and service, then, how can people have **Respect** for you? How can people believe in you? The forefront of this is credibility. How can your employees **Respect** you when you don't have **Respect** for them? You can't lead a team. You won't be able to convince them on your mission and you can't inspire them. There is no effective leadership if a leader can't align their values with organisational demands. Are your short-term and long-term values enshrined in **Respect** for others, or is it a narrow and personal agenda aimed at exploitation?

A leader must have a vision and believe in it. You must be the first person to believe in your vision, for if not then, how do you think another person can believe in it?

In Colin Powell's 'Thoughts on Leadership, from the book 'Developing Potential Across a full Range Of Leadership.' Cases on transactional and Transformational Leadership, Edited by Bruce J Avolio and Bernard M. Bass.

"... Leadership will always require people who have a vision of where they wish to take 'the led.' Leadership will always require people who are able to organise the effort of others to accomplish the objectives that flow from the vision. And leadership will always put a demand on leaders to pick the right people ... leadership also requires motivating people. And that means pushing the vision down to every level of the organisation. Leaders of this new industrial – information era have to be able to use these tools and understand the power of information and technology – and how that gives them new opportunities. ..But even more than as competitors, we should see our old enemies as markets. Information and technology allows you to do more 'niching.' Industry is discovering that the power of computer allows you to appeal to small and smaller markets because you are able to manufacture for smaller and smaller markets in an efficient and profitable way."

The first law of leadership demands that leaders select the best talent. If you're not able to do that, then you're not a leader. It is so vital that, if you miss out on this, then your vision will not be accomplished. How can you win when you got the wrong team in place? God asked Gideon to select his men by taking them to the stream. Anyone that does not drink water like a dog must be dropped. When I was growing up, I experienced one thing: My father, whom was a transporter, refused to pick me to be one of his drivers. He told me: "Emeka, you are not a competent truck driver. If I allow you to drive, then you will crash my vision." Selecting a bad team is the fastest way to crash your vision. You will never get where you are going with the bad team. Get the best talent who are ready to share your vision, and people who see their vision when they look at your own vision. These are people who see their vision as inextricably tied to yours as a leader. Just as God has tied all human destiny: "..their destiny is tied up with our destiny and our freedom is inextricably bound to our freedom." a line from Martin Luther's great speech.

As a leader, you must make people understand that your vision and theirs are tied together until you find that common ground. You cannot motivate people; that is what I suppose Colin Powell meant when he said: "..pushing the vision down to every level of the organisation." As a leader, your vision must resonate with others. It must resonate with your employees, and they must see the benefits beyond the money that is paid to them.

For instance, we have C. Hub magazine. It's beyond the magazine that you touch. It is a dream which we are selling. Unless we can put aside our differences, we cannot realise the vision in which the magazine has painted. By singularly hiring the best talent, you are motivating and pushing the vision down to the ordinary man in the street. You are connecting everyone and sowing the seed of healthy competition. This is necessary in creating a vibrant society or organisation, where leadership doesn't just come from the top but from many people in different positions. Great leaders believe it's better to ask for forgiveness than to ask for permission.

BUILDING ON OUR STRENGTH: CONVERTING SAUL TO PAUL

It says in the Bible: "all things work for good to them that believe."

Success is all about attitude. The kind of mindset you have will determine how you interpret your environment. *Your ability to see challenges in life as opportunity is the key.* From the way you take rejection to the way you take advantages of things all come into play. Converting all negative things to positive. One day, I was asked to cover a shift for a colleague of whom I thought was less busy. For some reason, however, I was called to cover for him. I had already planned how I was going to use the coming hours to my advantage. My plan was shattered when I was designated to take the shift. I felt terribly upset. Then, I remembered this principle of converting things from negative to positive. I regained myself and my adrenaline came down. Instantly, an idea surfaced and I used that time creatively. We lose a lot of positive energy when we moan and whinge over things that have not gone our way, especially things that we will still do after complaining and swearing. Think how best you can creatively use that time to enrich yourself. Remember, the longest in one's life is always the day you get upset. God uses this principle all the time. Look at Saul, for instance. To many, he was a challenge, but God focused only on his strength (despite his weaknesses). Saul, who was one of the most dangerous men on the planet, became Paul to become the most powerful preacher that changed the world completely. Look at winter. It's such an uncomfortable climate, yet it's one of the biggest elements to western civilisation. They converted it to something that many admire and look forward to each year. Never underestimate the power of seeing things through a rose colour spectacle. You're best when you focus on people's strengths and not their weaknesses; the positive side of life rather than the negative. Even in our talent, we must focus on our best, rather than on the things of which we are limited.

Note:

- Make the most with the least cost.
- 97% of the people who quit too soon are employed by the 3% that never gave up.
- Your past does not determine who you are.
- Your past prepares you for who your future.

We're not able to take risks in order to escape our unfulfilling jobs. We are bound by our own past, especially the choices we made through education or what we were taught. Something deep in our personal history that is embedded into one career. Humans are not excellent judges of future, interest and characters.

We have to be like a child in order to be successful, according to Jesus Christ.

A child is not worried about their past. We find ourselves in a constant struggle with our pasts, unable to make a decision. We have to try something new because of allegiance to the person we were rather than to the person we hope to become.

A.C Grayling said: "If there is anything worth fearing in the world, it is living in such a way that gives one cause for regret in the end."

Three things I have to focus on as I am writing this book of success:

1. flowers
2. child
3. Mohammed Ali

You need to be focused, as distraction could mean deception. Life begets life. Energy creates energy. It is by spending oneself that one becomes rich. Security is mostly a superstition. It does not exist in nature, nor do the children of men as a whole experience it. Avoiding danger is no safer in the long run than outright exposure . Life is either a daring adventure or nothing.

The greatest evil is not what one receives from the other, but the disservice one does to themselves.

Life is about defining a problem and finding a solution. Be consistent, create a context and focus on your goal.

FOCUS

Power of Focus

I always tell people, it's important to be a winner; use the principle of focus. People underrate its power because they don't understand it. As children we used to place a magnifying lens under a dried paper. We did this to focus the rays of sunlight onto the paper. And, within a short time, the paper will catch fire. This illustrates the power of focus. Be focused in what you are doing and you prove your critics wrong. Never allow people to distract you. It can only take distraction to defeat a person of focus. A man achieves whatever he makes his focus; this is the power of it.

It's not the size of a dog that matters it is the fight in a dog. I saw a goat that challenged a big cow, both engaged in a locking of horn. The goat will resist the cow locking in its horn and the cow will use its horn to fling the goat out after a sustained battle. The goat will not flinch or give up. It was determined to go against this beast 50 times its weight. They continued until the cow got tired and threw in its towel. One thing I observed the goat was doing: Hitting the big cow at one SPOT on its forehead. By focusing on that it was able to overpower the big cow. This shows that you achieve a giant stride with determination and focus. Men of Babel achieved great success because they had focus.

You are unstoppable and unbeatable if you can focus. The principle focus makes it possible to cut through a metal using a concentrated streams of water. Distractions are major stumbling blocks. By focusing you can prioritise, strategize and develop appropriate mindset to achieve your goals.

Have a look at a glass of water. Be critical about it. You will observe that the glass is half-full. When you take it to another person, he will probably say: "It is half-empty." So, you can see the difference in perception, due to point of focus. What is it that are you focusing on? The problem is that majority of people focus on the empty part of the glass without concentrating on the water in the glass. Remember, whatever you focus on expands. Why does one focus on the empty part of the glass? We have to focus on our strengths rather than on our weaknesses. If one focuses on their weaknesses, it is like focusing on nothing, and what is the result? Clearly one does not get anything. For one to be effective, they have to focus on their strengths. Focus is the key.

Your success is largely dependant on your ability to focus. Not being focused is a strategic error. The power to overcome the natural human tendency puts us ahead. We need to train ourselves to jump and leave the edge. Whatever one focuses on, one becomes the best at. Whatever one focuses on, one becomes. This is what makes lion the king of the jungle. If you focus on what is in your control, other things not in your control will fall in place. Focus is like setting an objective and obstacle will give way.

It is vital that you focus only on the positive. Focus only on the strengths. When you focus only on the positives, then you are a winner!

CHANGE

Change is an opportunity to get engaged and be successful. The first principle of success is change. Unless we understand what change means then, we'll always frown at it. Change provides us time to try again and be as successful as we were born to be. Change is the generous opportunity provided by God to fulfill our purpose. Change validates the principle that we are created to be highly successful in all we do. Change teaches us how to be competitive in every part of our lives.

The change of pause, the change of time, and the change of seasons offer us new beginning. It brings about new ways of doing things and new era. Change is synonymous to success. We must embrace change because it works in our favour. We cannot carry on with business as usual and expect a positive result.

For instance, social media provided a leverage for us to be in the business of magazine publication, given our origins. Social media took everybody by storm and changed the entire business landscape. We did not wait or frown, whine and moan about the change but we took the change as an advantage. Social media helped us to see things in a different way and discover a better way of doing things.

We need to change the ways we do things in order to produce the desired result. Unless we change, our ways we will never be successful. Unless the seasons change, the trees cannot be fruitful. Albert Einstein says: ' "Doing the same thing over and over again and expecting different results is insanity. If we must always re-introduce energy, creativity, strategy, tactics, to our thinking, actions, product and service, then we will always be successful."

Look at Steve Jobs. In the new millennium, he boldly introduced the iPod, smart phones and the tablets. This completely changed how we listen to music and speak on the phone. And persistently, they've been changing and introducing new concepts to the products. In the same vein, the way we look at ourselves and other people and products should change if we can actually want to get grip of what we are doing.

The first step towards success is this, you must reclaim yourself. You have to get rid of the wrong beliefs and mindsets that have been preventing you from achieving success. Such as: fear, pointing the finger, fear of criticism, what people are going to say, what family members do and if they're not interested in your vision, whinging, moaning indecision, laziness and procrastination. Then, replace them with wisdom, power, love, respect, self-will, gratitude and vision. Clear the clutter. This is essential. You can't be making the same mistakes over and over and expect different results. You can't seek permission to go after your dreams and you can't seek approval from anyone to free yourself.

When we started our business of publishing, many of my friends and others in the industry felt bad that we did not seek approval from them. Remember the area is not a new area. People have being doing business before you.

According to Albert Einstein, doing the same thing over and over and expecting a different result is insanity. "I'm a mover and a shaker. The movers and shakers are all about change. Not doing things the way they've always been done, or keeping your head below the parapet."

TIME & PERFECT TIMING

A man who dares to waste one hour of his time has not yet discovered the value of life. **Charles Darwin**

Time offers us the opportunity to introduce the change necessary for us to be successful. The pulsation of our heart offers the time to bring about the changes we require all the time. The movement of the sun, the movement of time brings in the change in circumstances. In between the pulsation of time is the change and this change is the opportunity. Time provides us this fantastic opportunity to embrace the changes necessary to be successful. Time provides us with ample opportunity to introduce the changes which we desire to be successful. We have to understand that clinging onto one thing is helpful as we shift our priorities and perspectives.

You must understand time and respond to it. Just like the trees respond to seasons, we must take advantage of the time. Time is as essential as when to introduce the desired change. There is a saying that without time everything will happen at the same time. There would be chaos and disorderliness.

Let's understand what timing is. One day a pastor explains timing to his congregation. He brought in three members to the pulpit, a lady and two boys. He gave the two boys a long rope to start skipping while the lady was to jump in. The first time the lady attempted to jump in, she got the timing wrong. This stalled the continuous spinning of the rope. She then jumped out and started to observe the spinning again. The second time she got herself ready. As soon as the rope swung tangential to the floor, she quickly jumped in. When she jumped in, she continued jumping up and down and followed the pace of the rope. She can only stop when the two boys stopped skipping. So, the continuous pulse in our heart and the movement of sun indicates that we are not done. We are only done when our heart stops pumping or the movement of sun stops and as we can see they have not stopped.

Another aspect of time that is necessary is what I call, 'flogging a dead horse', because a dead horse is the horse whose time has passed. One cannot take the world back to the era of horse and cart. The world is only interested in efficient and effective use of its scarce resources hence cost effective. Understanding of our time and era would help you in deciding the kind of business one has to go into and how one should run their business. For instance, it is not cost effective to go into the old Kodak polaroid picture of 70s. You will not only be losing money, but you will be 'flogging a dead horse.' Today we are looking at how we perceive ourselves, other people, products and services. This will help us maximise profit in business. The 3R of business success: re-assessing oneself, people, products and services to extract energy which we have for centuries left untapped.

Martin Luther says time is always ripe to do what is right. How we value our time determines where we are going. If we don't have value for time, then we won't be able to make the most of it. What we do with our time today determines what our tomorrow will be.

To an extent, God has given us power to predict our future. Our destiny is in our hands. This is the extent of how God loves us. We can always shape our future by what we do today. Remember, we are our thoughts. That is the sort of power of which God has provided for us.

If you want to do things, then begin right now. Do not wait till tomorrow because tomorrow does not belong to anyone but God. He chooses to give it to anyone He wants to give it. Don't postpone the decision to carry out your plans today. Make that timely, profitable or strategically sound decision today.

Our sense of whether we have time enough is dependent on how we think about time. Do we see things from objective point of view or subjective point of view? Do we see the glass as half-full or half-empty? By choosing to think differently, we can transform our feelings about the same objective facts.

Timing is critical in all you are doing. People who understand time are very smart. Your ability to know when to invest, and when not to, is critical. We have seasons and time. We have to observe these before we jump into a business. Successful people look before they leap. People who shoot moving objects will have to time them before shooting! Everything on the surface of the earth happens with time. If one does not time things properly, then they miss the target; they only have themselves to blame. Business is all about perfect timing.

ATTITUDE

Jesse Owens wouldn't have achieved that great feat without mastering himself and putting up an attitude different from other athletes. It's an attitude of fair-play.

The attitude we choose determines how successful we become. The system may be unfavourable to you, but with a right attitude you will upturn things to become a winner. Without a positive attitude, life becomes drudgery, painful and difficult. You can change negative thinking into positive thinking with the right attitude. Attitude is a reflection of your inside. You will find it difficult to understand **The Big R of a Successful Business** if, you don't understand 'Attitude.' Respect for oneself, people and products hinges on it. The best way to succeed is the choice you make. If we choose to take a good attitude to what we do, which obviously come from our mind, then we can melt down a huge amount of difficulty in front of us. Attitude is not just about deep source of energy or creativity, but that passion which excites and motivates us.

According Steve Redgrave, rapport between Jesse Owens and Luz Long, African-Americans and Germans demonstrated how a good attitude can melt away huge prejudice and propaganda of the white supremacism of Hitler. Both Owens and Long shared tactical thoughts and warmed up to each other that made the whole thing unimaginable. Owens said, *"What I remember most was the friendship I struck up with Luz Long, the German jumper. He was my strongest rival, yet it was he who advised me to adjust my run-up in the qualifying round and thereby helped me to win. Our friendship was important to me."*

Respect for person and good attitude can make a difference to what we achieve and how we achieve it. Talent was not enough in Owens case, for he wisely wove in attitude and talent to become the best sprinter of his generation. In the subsequent chapters, we will be talking about the discovering of oneself and respect to other people even your strongest rivals, critics and your competitors as demonstrated by the story of Jesse Owens and Luz Long. The greatest attitude is one of making it happen – put it into action. Practise it and not just saying it. It is said that "a bad attitude is like a flat tire, you can't go anywhere until you've changed it."

If you have a right attitude to time, you are more likely to believe that you have enough time to do what you want to do. A friend once said to me: your contentment to life depends on how you see it. This is unshakeable, and not dependant on whether you see life as a privilege or a right. How do you see life: subjectively or objectively? Do you see the glass as half-full or half-empty. From a narrow perspective or a wider perspective? Do you see things only in black and white? What is our outlook? Lewis Hamilton did not make it only by talent and determination, but something greater than that. Hamilton's attitude took him to that level: World Class Formula One Driver. You have a vision; what do you do? You know you have to stay calm, cool and collected—even under pressure and opposition to see it work. Jesus showed a positive attitude even in the face of death, a demeanor that is mixed with humility and creativity. Why does one exhibit this rare attitude? Because you know your vision: Where you are going.

A dancer once said, *"As a dancer, you don't accept "No." I was like that as a child when doing shows – I never took a day off. Her body is representative of who she is and how hard she works – her discipline is beyond belief. She taught me it's about always asking questions, finding solutions, doing something new, wanting to be different and pushing the boundaries. All this makes up who I am, because she's trained me to think that way: So much so that she has taught herself about anatomy and Physiology:* **"I've studied Chakras and found out about energy balance. We don't talk about emotions because that's not how society works, but we all store them up – and the people I train kept coming up with the same (Emotion – based) problem. Dance has always been my way to release emotions, and I've always felt very powerful and healthy afterwards."**

The attitude is being great at whatever you do. Your mental attitude will make success a certainty. You've got to have unshakeable belief in yourself. From the above one can see that we are taught not to show emotion, encouraged to keep our emotions under wraps. They say if you want to develop excellence in big things in life, then you must develop habits in little matters. Habit is an attitude.

RESILIENCE

Your Ability To Bounce Back

Most people don't succeed in life because they gave up sooner than they should have. One only fails when they give up, but as long as you keep doing what you are doing (and not giving up), then you are up and running. I assure you that you are a winner. It is important that you understand and weigh things before you start because, if you are not convinced about the goal or the purpose of your pursuit, when the 'chips are down', you find yourself on the run. Sometimes fear induces people to surrender. When you meet people who believe 'no retreat no surrender' is such a powerful thing, then you cannot defeat them because they're always there. Resilience is a very 'beautiful and handsome' quality that distinguishes people from others. It's a great quality that takes people very far in life. For me, the main reason people fail in life is that they're not resilient.

Serena Williams reminisces on her success as Tennis number one, she said; "20 years ago, I played my first professional Tennis match. I was 14. I was scared. I was not prepared for the stage. But determined, I went on. Butterflies consumed my stomach leaving no space for me to eat, to prepare for my match. Less than an hour later I left the court devastated in defeat. A6 – 1, 6 – 1 loss to Annie Miller. Basically she crushed me. Not only did I look like a novice but I looked like I did not belong anywhere on the court. However, born with an innate insatiable desire to never quit. I knew I would return. I would come back, I could not predict that I would win 21 Gram Slam titles and be number one in the world even 20 years later, but I tell you this: never give up on your dreams. It may not happen when you want it to but, one day your knight in shining armour will come true if you keep going. I leave you with this. Be positive and above all be humble."

Indeed, no one can thwart the purposes of your mind – for they can't be touched by fire, steel, tyranny, slander, or anything. **Marcus Aurelius**

Challenges and obstacles are part of life. Things could be tough and unpredictable but nothing can stop you. Nothing can resist human mind. Firstly, God lives inside you. Secondly, every course of action has what is termed as 'a reverse clause." A reverse clause is a kind of a backup plan or option. For instance, you are subjected to a difficult situation like prison or expelled from school. Instead of the chain of events to break, demoralised, anger, frustrate you, rather you refuse to be broken by the difficult conditions. You learn patience, act of forgiveness and continue in the direction you have set out. The reverse clause is the patience, forgiveness and the act of starting afresh. This experience will embolden you to continue in the direction you have already started. All you need is to focus on the vision. Keep on going. It won't take long before you achieve your dream.

PERSISTENCE

You cannot defeat a person who never gives up. **Faustina Anyanwu**

A persistent person does not accept no for an answer. He is like a salesperson. You say 'NO' to them, they continue! Again you say 'NO' to them they continue! You say 'NO' to them they continue! They don't give up. They interpret 'NO' as wait! Persistent people know that nothing can stand on their way. They're very positive and optimistic that they will succeed. Nothing will ever stop them. They stand against all oppositions. Neither fear of today, nor worries of tomorrow, can stop a persistent person. Not even power of hell can stop one in pursuing their purpose. They know they have to shine their light. At this point, they know that their purpose is not negotiable and, therefore, they pursue their vision and purpose with passion and persistence. Persistent people are excited with opposition and resistance along their road to their vision. They understand that what they are born to do is always locked behind closed doors. You've got to knock and knock before the door is opened. Dr Myles said: "Whatever you are born to do will never be given to you. You have to go and get it. Again, whatever you are born to do will not be easy even though it is simple." You must be a transformed person in order to accomplish that for which you were born to do. You've got to surrender gracefully things of your youth in order to deliver on this mission. I love what St Paul said: "To be transformed by renewing of your mind."

Let us not become weary in doing good, for at the proper time we will reap a harvest if we do not give up. **Galatians 6:9**

This story told by Jesus illustrates persistence. "Suppose one of you has a friend and he goes to him at midnight and says: ' Friend, lend me three loaves of bread because a friend of mine on a journey has come to me. I have nothing to set before him.' The one inside answers, 'Don't bother me. The door is already locked, and my children are with me in bed. I can't get up and give anything.' I tell you, though he will not get up and give him the bread he is his friend, yet because of the man's boldness he will get up and give him as much as he needs." The man got what he wanted because he was persistent.

Ask and it will be given to you. Seek you will find. Knock and the door will be opened. Ask, Seek, and Knock all has persistence in them. You've got to be highly persistent. One has to understand that every idea or view we have now, was once seen as eccentric.

Do not fear to be eccentric in opinion, for every opinion now accepted was once eccentric. **Bertrand Russell**

At first, people will reject your view. Likewise, people will reject you. But you have to persist, because only you know where you are coming from. You are the one who has the vision and you know it is not hoax; you believe in it. Remember that saying: "The stone which the builders have rejected has become the cornerstone of the house." When it comes to the society, the society already have a script for you to act out. When you reject it, they will reject you. It is your responsibility to stick to the script given to you by God. You have to reject the script foisted on you by the society.

CONSISTENCY

And now, little children, abide in Him, that when He appears, we may have confidence and not be ashamed before Him at His coming. **1 John 2:28**

The word abide means to accept or act in accordance with someone/thing. It tells one to be consistent or continue with something. Consistency is a word many love. I love constant supply of electricity, water and all good things. We love consistency we love strikers that are consistent, basketball players like Lebron James, Michael Jordan. These are people who are consistent in what they do. Jesus Christ was consistent with his prayers at early rise of sun everyday, and was consistent in what He did.

Consistency is so important in life and business that without it one cannot be successful. Any inch one drops in not being consistent will instantly be taken by the competitors, opponents, critics, rivals, enemies nature does not allow vacuum. The reason they are not far away is that they are around the corner. Consistency as a principle is highly important: #Keepwalking and #keepgoing. Consistency gets one to end. Consistency gets one to the finish line.

Aristotle said: "We are repeatedly what we do." As we all love consistency. The question becomes: "Are we consistent in what we do?

It is very difficult to be consistent in what we do that made John the Apostle use the word abide in Him. Be consistently in love with Him. If anyone can be consistent in his work, then they are winners. If one can grow in consistently honing their talent they become unstoppable. Being successful is about being consistent in doing what you love, regardless of challenges and obstacles. To be consistent in what one does demands discipline and understanding; one has to be transformed. Once transformed, one cannot return to the formal old ways of doing things. If one is not consistent, they've not transformed and, hence, one cannot be said to be successful. According to St. Paul: "To be transformed, you have to continuously renew your mind. This is about consistency. Consistent in the art of renewing your mind. Consistent in being engaged and involved brings in the right transformation. *Look at the Butterfly, once transformed will never return to Larva or Caterpillar.*

*If you understand the principles in this book, you will **Respect** them. You become successful because you are a transformed person.*

DISCIPLINE

You have to be quite disciplined and focused. It must be anchored in your values. People who are disciplined achieve success and they are admired. They are perfectly equipped for their purpose. Discipline is knowledge. It is vital if one has to apply all the concepts and ideas that one develops in life. One may have all knowledge, but without discipline one cannot benefit from this knowledge. One cannot go through the transformation necessary to become successful. For instance, Lisa Nichols says: 'I was willing to completely die to any form of me I have been; so that I can birth the woman I was becoming. The reason why a lot of people won't become who they want is because they become too attached to whom they have always been.'

You need discipline to change that form of you which you have always. Just like yam, to produce new one, it has die of the older one. We need change the older habits and beliefs and values we have for us to become who we want to be. To become who we are created to be. What you are given is hidden. Whatever you are born to be will never be given to you. Whatever you are born to be, you've got to get out and and get it. Whatever you are born to be will never come to you easy. It all require discipline.

> **Blessed are the meek, for they will inherit the earth. Matt 5:5**

Meek here means discipline, controlled will. The meek means highly disciplined.
   Love this:

> **If, then, you have not been faithful in the unrighteous wealth, who will entrust to you the true riches? Luke 16:11**

One needs to be accountable and be self-disciplined with talent and money. All responsibilities you are given must be accounted. If you are not responsible, how will God reward you favourably? The poor always have a false concept about money. You have seen that if you're not prudent in managing money and other gifts from God, God will not reveal to you, your true riches. We have misconception about money. How can the wealth of the wicked be transferred to the righteous? It cannot be transferred if we view money as evil or satanic. Jesus told you, 'children of Light in Luke 16, to go and learn from the people of the world on how to manage ie "Parable Of The Shrewd Manager." He taught you wisdom, you don't understand, but people of this world practise it.' He said, 'go and learn from them.' Clearly Jesus was asking you to do what Joseph did. Joseph worked with the wicked Pharaoh in the Bible. He did not reject working for him because he was wicked and evil. Worship of money is evil.

Anything human exalted is abomination before God.

We need to control the child in us, teach him to be disciplined.

"Loving a child doesn't mean giving in to all his whims; To love him is to bring out the best in him, to teach him to love what is difficult."
Nadia Boulanger

DECISION

***First they ignore you, then they laugh at you, then they fight you, then you win.* Mahatma Gandhi**

Many people contemplate actions, but only few to take decision to take action. Leadership is about making decision. I'm one the people that find it difficult to make decisions. I defer, procrastinate, and delay action; this is a hell of a problem for me. The conflict between Spirit and body leads to doubts, fear and ignorance. Making a decision promptly is vital. Much more important is that if you fail to take decision the universe will take decision for you – not making a decision is a decision in itself.

Great MLK said: "Time is ripe to do what is right." So long as what you want to do is a right thing, the time is always okay to do it. Again when it comes to your purpose time is always ripe to start. I have never seen anything like 'DOING.' What matters is what you have done. My eyes opened when I went to the hospital for my appendix and I ended up in having a kidney failure. I wept. When I saw my young wife and three girls, it was too unthinkable. It was like Jonah who stayed in a belly of a fish for 3 days and 3 nights. The question becomes: "Why do we never expect unexpected events in our lives?

For me, it was a warning shot from God to reveal to me there is no time in this world. Once something is right, fire on. You've got a message from God – a still, small voice inside you. You must listen to it. "I shall lose my usefulness the moment I stifle the still small voice." That was what Gandhi said. This is non-negotiable.

The only way to be relevant is to be creative. This is your choice. To make heir while the sunshines. There comes a time when no one can work. This is why you must take a decision. As long as you have breath inside of you, start your purpose. You have limited time on earth. Anything you don't do while you are still alive you cannot do it again. God desperately needs you to do things now. We often defer decisions because we have doubts and fears. Doubt is dangerous . Never have doubt because you have God inside you; nothing is impossible. Decision making involves risks, change and consequences. Our default position is to stay in our comfort zone or to freeze and say God will do it. We don't realise that God cannot do for you, for that which He can do with you and also that which He can do through you.

Fear and ignorance can keeps us in a rat race and prevents us from making decisions. No wonder many contemplate action and never carry it out. Decision making is complex. It involves questioning and upsetting status quo and people don't like that. We live in an interdependent world where your decisions can affect the next person. Once you make a decision, you gonna get to the middle ground or chasm where you get armies of critics who are determine to ignore you, laugh at you, fight you but if you persist you win. There is a saying: "What you hear, you forget; what you see, you remember and what you do, you understand." The test of understanding is in doing it. You can only understand something when you do it.

Look at Edison; he had to try 999 times before he produced electric bulb. In-between the first trial and the 999th one, what do you think he was doing? He was experimenting time after time. He did one, and it did not work. He learnt from the previous trial, acted on the feedback and continued. Each one he did understand things and he continued trying to better it. Having improved on the last one, he tried again. At that point, many people will ask you to stop. Yet, he did not quit.

Next look at the Wright brothers; why did achieve their result? Many people who tried before them failed because they were not persistent and were not thinking outside the box. According to Sam L. Savage, the author of 'The Flaw Of Averages.'

So, why did their plane fly while so many before them stayed on the ground? In a word, models. A critical insight occurred, for example, when Wilbur sat idly twisting a long thin bicycle inner tube box with the ends torn out. Suddenly, he realised that the same principle could be applied to warp the wings of an airplane to make it turn right or left. The two brothers immediately built a kite to test this concept, which was one of the cornerstones of their design. Thus, the first model of the first airplane was a bicycle inner tube box. Before they achieved the initial flight, they had built many more models, including several unpowered gliders that they flew themselves.'

The only way to control the big ship is to get it going. The only to understand something is to start doing it. You can't control a ship that is stationary. I never set to write, 'The Big 'R' Of A Successful Business.' It all began when I was writing an article for the website, and along the line I got stuck and I called a friend for help. Mr Kevin Reddy gave an insight. Then, instantly I realised I could write a book based on this insight. So, doing something is the secret of success.

SELF-ESTEEM

What is the image you have of yourself? When you look in the mirror, what do you see? Image of who do you see? This is where your self-esteem comes from. What are you made of? What do you believe in? What are your experiences in life? Do you remember all the challenges you have literally overcome? What are your strengths? Do you believe that all things are possible? These are what give you self-esteem.

Imagine when you understand that God is your rock and your root. Who can shake you? The environment and temperature can change, seasons can change, and you will be there like an evergreen tree planted near the river. Self-esteem is critical to self-confidence. Without self-esteem, you cannot have self-confidence. Self-esteem is what people don't see that lies within you. What they see on the surface is self-confidence. When you remember the difficult battles you have won in your life or the past experiences and how you solved your problems, then your self-esteem begins to grow. When you have that image of God, there will be no room for devil. Once you give room to the devil, it comes in. Instantly your heart and mind become infested with the spirit of fear. This is obviously is not from God.

There is a saying: "When you start to walk back, then you are showing the devil the way." I see self-esteem as the invisible of my being that gives rise to self-confidence. Lack of personal self-esteem leads to self-protective and overly competitive tendencies. Without self-esteem, one cannot cultivate interpersonal skills and leads to excessive self-preservation.

Your self-image determines how you see the world.

We are the reflection of image we have inside us. Result speaks for itself. If you look into the mirror and the image you see is not what you like, what do you do? Obviously you change the image by working on your physical self. So, if you don't like the result you are getting in life, then you change what is inside of you. You work on your self-esteem. Low self-esteem is like a paradigm which one needs to break off from. The images, values, stories and beliefs you have inside your subconscious mind about yourself make it impossible for you to have self-confidence. You must break away from this paradigm for you to have high self-esteem. This is what is called paradigm shift.

Remember:

Thoughts lead to feelings.

Feeling leads to actions.

Action leads to results.

Take self-esteem as the invisible and self-confidence as visible. The invisible controls the visible.

SELF-CONFIDENCE

Self-confidence is a result of self-esteem you have. The more self-esteem you have, then the more self-confidence you possess. Without self-confidence, you cannot do anything. That self-confidence is a feeling of self-belief that we have what it takes to do things irrespective of the challenges and obstacles. Irrespective of barrier and hurdles that you can deliver. Self-confidence is important when you are dealing with others to assure them that you know what you are doing at any given time. The more you build your self-belief, the more confident you become and the more successful you are. There is nothing you cannot achieve with self-confidence. Lack of confidence comes from fear. Fear of making mistakes and people laughing at you. Think of babies; do they care if people laugh at them or not? They don't feel humiliation; that is why they are able to talk and walk. We can learn anything in life. We have the capacity to acquire any skill because we are born with intense drive to learn. Never fear about making mistakes, for when you make a mistake you learn from it. That is the advantage of making mistakes.

According to Albert Einstein; "Anyone who never makes mistakes is one who has never tried new things." In fact, I cherish my children when they make mistakes because humans are full of imperfection. Fear of making mistakes is what kills off our creativity. We are so worried about what people, friends, and relatives will say. But this is not life; this is bondage. I always tell people don't put me in box, because if you do, I'm going to wriggle out. *Babies don't worry about making mistakes or humiliating themselves; this particular attitude makes them great. If you want to be great, then learn this quality from babies.* Believe in yourself, no matter what others might say. Believe in yourself when no one else does.

Any failures or mistakes you have are simply feedback. In that sense, you improve. Alter your brain: Anything you are afraid of or fear doing, do it. It is not a crime and you have not harmed or hurt anyone. Taking responsibility and action makes you gain self-confidence. You gain self-confidence by moving outside your comfort zone. Doing something unattainable is a way to overcome your obstacles, challenges and self-doubts. Insecurity is the opposite of self-confidence. The secret of success is self-confidence. Always be in control of what you are doing. I learnt this when I was learning how to drive. Driving is all about being in control the car. Low self-esteem does not give you self-confidence. If you don't have confidence, then work on your self-esteem. We can see self-confidence here.

One day I asked Faustina a question about CN Nwagwu, that prompted us to search in Google. The result showed nil. We searched 3 good times, while his titles nothing showed.

At this point, you see a kind of fog. Next you abandoned search without searching with a different title. Faustina, who was doing the search, knew that her uncle was a Director of Domestic operations. For the fact it was not written or the search proved nil does mean it can't be done. To any soul without confidence, that was the end of the road. It was a red flag. Time to end it. Imagine when God met the earth without form and void, and darkness was over the face of the deep. That point was the point to quit, but God continued because He is a confident God.

In the same vein, when Faustina got to the point which I termed as fog, because she has confidence in herself.

1. She knew that it was true
2. She can construct that image – get all information she needed.

What did she do? She began to piece together all information one by one. It did not take long before she made contact with the man's children. Further, she called her mum and auntie here who helped in providing more information for her to construct and write a brilliant article about CN Nwagwu. To me, this is what self-confidence is all about— the ability to initiate and execute a project, while meeting and exceeding the target. There's no need to be afraid, or doubt but fold your sleeves get on with the job and finish it in an unflappable manner. Challenges can't be greater than your purpose. Jesus was very confident because he knew how things were made, he knew their end. So to begin it, he knew what the result would be.

Self-confidence is a key to success and lack of confidence can become a self-fulfilling prophecy.

Marcus Garvey said: "If you have no confidence in self, you are twice defeated in the race of life."

PRAYERS

I have said, ye are gods; and all of you are children of the most High. **Psalm 82:6**

Prayer is talking to God. One of the greatest arsenals God gave man is the art of prayer. I strongly believe that whatever we pray for has been granted by God. Word of God cannot return void. God has raised His word above every other thing. Faith to believe that it has been granted is highly vital in this case. You cannot come to God without faith. Jesus Christ taught us how to pray. We learnt that Jesus was always praying and usually starts his day with prayers. He usually starts prayer as early as the sunrise. Whatever you pray for through our Lord Jesus Christ, it will always be answered. If you did not get answer, that means you doubted. Lack of faith makes our prayers not to come through. Prayer is so powerful that, whatever you bind here on earth, the Heavens will listen. Elijah prayed and there was no rain in Israel for 3 years. After that, he prayed again. The Heavens opened up and rain began to fall. Joshua prayed and the sun stood still. This is how powerful we are. You should always remember the powers you have. You should always remember how powerful you are. Don't forget you are a child of God and nothing is impossible to you.

*Therefore I tell you, whatever you ask for in prayer, believe that
you have received it, and it shall be yours.* **Mark 11:24**

*The major weakness of most humans is that they recognise the obstacle they
must surmount without recognising the spiritual power at their command
by which those obstacles may be removed at their command.* **Unknown**

There is nothing we can do without God. With God all things are possible.
With God on our side, we can surmount any obstacle or challenges in this
world. Jesus reminds us to pray all the time. At Gethsemane, he told his
apostles to watch and pray because he knew how important and powerful it
is to pray. There was a time the weight of death became overwhelming for
Jesus; he cried to His everlasting father. He said: "If it is your will, then let
this cup pass over me." At this critical point, one cannot help but pray to God
for reinforcement. It was said that Jesus was sweating blood to illustrate the
level of suffering. When we encounter similar situations, we have to fall back
on God through no other way but prayers to renew our mind and spirit. One
of ways to describe Jesus Christ is 'prayer.'

Prayer should be our second nature. During sham, broken dreams and
drudgery prayer are vital to lead us through the bumpy and rocky road of
life. Prayer keeps you in communion with the one who gave your purpose
and vision. People will abandon you, your friends and relatives will go, and
you find yourself lonely as you start building your business. Yet, you don't
have to give up. You've got to pray and persist; you will definitely win.

UNDERSTANDING THE BIG R
OF A SUCCESSFUL BUSINESS

*If want to look at anything, there's only one thing I check out for: The EUS(
Essential Underlying Spirit) and this gives rise to RESPECT.*

Life is beautiful, but who can see the beauty? At dawn, the sun begins to
break through the gloom changing the entire landscape. Introducing fresh
wind of joy and happiness on our shores. It feeds our tender imagination
with a feeling of wonders and awe. The newly – gained serenity evaporating
and powering all things to come alive to make a difference

We've been equipped to thrive and excel in all manners of endeavours from birth. We've been given the most powerful tool by God – the brain and a soul to develop self-will to make great choices in life. Exercising this choice is important if one has to be successful in life. It starts with self-belief. It's that person who understands himself that becomes successful. If you believe in yourself, then anything becomes possible. Success in business is about attitude and habits and all is wrapped in one word – RESPECT and this book is a journey of self-discovery.

When one develops, RESPECT for self, RESPECT for people, RESPECT for their products and services, it becomes imperative for them to be successful in their business. This concept comes with the hard skills essential for the day to day running of your business. When you embrace the concept of **The Big R of a successful business**, then you become confident and aware that the need for success is stronger than the fear of failure. When you have respect for yourself, you begin to understand your purpose. Likewise, you understand your goal and mission and why success is on the line. You must not fail, nor must you quit or slack off. When you have a mission, obstacles are no longer a problem. When you understand yourself, you'll embrace the word RESPECT. Life is about competition and the one who plays better wins. For you to win, you must not only understand the rule of the game but must be applied. If you ingrain RESPECT in your work and aspiration success comes naturally; hard skills also become reality.

Everyone wins if you appreciate yourself, people, products and services.

To thrive and grow to the best of one's ability, we must learn to **RESPECT** oneself in order to tap into one's inner power.

When you fail to understand yourself, then you will appear to people and your staff as opinionated, domineering and bossy.

In an article written by Lucy Kellaway On Work on Financial Times Monday 18, May 2015 pg12 that Tim Armstrong CEO of AOL is "living proof that it is nonsense to argue that most successful leader are humble ones.

Step 1: The writer says the AOL boss is clumsy, ungrammatical and plain baffling. On various occasions, I've given him gongs for misuse of language, but he goes on excelling.

Having a respect for oneself, people and products doesn't mean you have to put on a personality of another. You must be proficient in a language for you to be successful in your business. All he has to show is that he can connect with himself, people and his product and services. The coining of a new verb – to game – change. All depends on the context and the audience.

Step 2: "There was the even more famous way. He fired an employee in front of 1,000 others simply because he had had the nerve to take the photograph."

Dismissing a staff whom he deemed to have ignored the culture of the company – ethics, values, belief and images for their personal interest. This shows the employee is more of an outsider than an insider. The culture of AOL ought to have been communicated and properly understood by the culprit. Having a respect involves both the bosses and employees knowing what to do at each point in time. The interest of business must come before their personal interest. Employers and employees must know the vision, mission and purpose of the business and must be ingrained in the products and services.

Step 3: If you listen to the tape of the firing, you will notice that the truly awful thing was not merely that he sacked someone in public for nothing. It was the way he talks to employees. A hectoring monologue, in the course of which he twice tells people if they don't agree with him they can leave right way.

We do regard having respect for someone means you have to compromise and pally along with people who do not have respect for themselves and not talk of the respect for their company or business. Leaders sometimes break rules, especially when it comes to taking decisions and sending direct and clear message that they know what they are doing. It is necessary to erase doubts, ignorance and fear and bring in confidence and optimism. Leadership is not followership. It's about doing the right thing that is in line with the vision and success of a business.

Step 4: Tim Armstrong reveals that his Dad was a Vietnam vet who gave his son some uncompromising advice when he took on AOL: "Do whatever it takes to be successful."

When one slips into the mantle of leadership, the first thing that come to their mind is: "What will I do to be successful?" The grotesque picture the writer wants us to have of the AOL boss is that of opinionated, domineering and authoritative person. He is one who can do anything, including ignoring the feelings of the staff. In ideal situations, the interest of the owners of a business and employees should be identical so that they can succeed in the business. What leaders should always do is to continue to communicate the vision of the company to staff and people who come in contact with the products and services. But this cannot be done if the business owners do not understand themselves, the people, products and services. This is why **The Big R of a successful business** goes into detail to explain the principles behind a successful business.

We need to define what we mean by a successful business. Success in business is not that of Lehman brothers, Enron or Murdock kind of business. The success in business we mean here is a narrow definition, by which it does not involve the throwing around of money. It involves manipulations that we see, which brought the banking crisis of 2008. We are talking of businesses whose foundation is built on ethics and integrity, images, trust and authenticity. These are what makes businesses sustainable and strong. Businesses that give the owners, workers and people happiness, which centers their lives.

Success in business is important because it brings influence and result. This is one of the ways that we fulfil our purpose, mission and vision.

It's one of the ways we transfer our talents, image, beliefs and all what we have to the new generations.

MINDSET

Mindset is vital if we must be successful. The man who was given one talent; what was his mindset towards his master? That was the deadliest mindset one could have. One can't move an inch in life with such a mindset. What is your mindset to the giver? Do you feel that the giver did not give you enough or that the giver did not love you (or they ignored you)? If you don't have positive mindset, then you cannot learn. You cannot do business, nor can you take risk. You still have the mind of the past. Nothing more dangerous than living in the present with the mind of the past. You cannot go into adventure because your thinking is not positive. Success is about learning.

Success is about improving what we have and making things better. Life is not perfect, nor are institutions or politics. Imperfection is our world. The question now comes: What are your views of things? Do you see the glass of water from half-empty spectacles or half-full? These are what matter in life. Does one have the mindset that turns failure into success? Jesus Christ said: "Unless we receive the kingdom like a child... we will not enter heaven." This statement is loaded and powerful. The view one adopts profoundly affects them. It determines if one becomes what they want to be in life. It determines what kind of things you accomplish. A child is capable of learning how to walk and speak. This is, as a result, how they look at life. Children don't worry about making mistakes; neither do they see humiliation as something to worry about. The kind of mindset determines how you handle stress. A person with a powerful mindset is highly motivated by stress and difficult situations. They don't give up. They are not easily demotivated by factors that affect many. Just as a salesperson is capable of drawing a distinction between refusal of a product and rejection of self. Mindsets are just beliefs, in as much as they are powerful you change it. Wherever you want to go, you have to build up the mindset that will take you there. You got to have a mindset that is congruent to your vision. One that is capable of breaking through any gloom which you may face along your journey to realising your full potentials. A growth mindset that liberates one from bondage and fear, one that restores joy and happiness. A person with a growth mindset believes he can always be better. He can learn new things and improve their lives.

On the other hand, people with fixed mindset find it hard to go extra miles. They find it hard to stretch their knowledge because they worry more about what people will think of them. Ironically, the world doesn't necessarily care about what you think. According to Steven Pressfield: "It's not that people are mean or cruel, they're just busy." Yet, these busy people are the ones preventing you from going after things that matter to your heart and mind. This is ridiculous. Take on the mindset of what you want to become.

Don't allow the inner critic inside our head to run berserk. Anything one calls a disadvantage or handicap can always turn around to advantage. For example, a friend of mine who came into UK from Nigeria had difficulty regularising his papers. He managed to secure work with an agency, where he made more money than people who came in with visa. His secret was that he did not allow his status stop him from looking for job. He saw his handicap as an advantage and he proved it by what he achieved. Great achievers have positive mindset. They don't wallow in self-pity and self-doubt. They simply see it as strength and move forward. Before you realise it, they're at the top.

Zacchaeus, the short man in the Bible, did not see his height as a disadvantage. Rather, he took advantage of it by thinking of what he must do to see the Saviour. What did he do? He climbed the Sycamore tree and he met face to face with the Lord. The story is metaphorical. If you have any deficiency, then what do you do? You have to think outside the box. Ask yourself: what can I do? Instead of holding a pity party or running a negative movie in your head on and on. You always have a choice, because it is the greatest wealth God has given man, not life as we were meant to believe.

Zacchaeus had a choice of hiding at home whining and whinging and complaining. Instead, he took a chance and ignored what people will say. It's not what people say that matters. Rather, it is your purpose and personal assignment that matters most. He acted on his choice and climbed on a tree. That singular choice brought wealth, joy and happiness in his life.It is not life that matters but it is the choice you act on that matters. That is why people with positive mindsets achieve all they want to achieve. They know they have a choice to multiply their gift or not to multiply it. To sow a seed or not to sow, to invest or not to invest, to learn or not to learn. To be a giver or a receiver.

Why is a lion the king of the jungle? It's the mindset. One's mindset is beyond focus and self-awareness. Without a clear mindset, one cannot maximise their full potentials. One of the experiences I had working for my in-law was ability to develop a mindset. One day, he told me that I should have this mindset:

"Anyone coming into our office for money withdrawal is considered a thief until that person is gone through all the test to ascertain whether the card they possessed belong to them or not."

With that mentality, it is extremely difficult for any fraudster to beat in the game. This is the mindset we were operating on to thwart any plan from the bad guys defrauding us. Another coach instructing his team on how keep an office safe said:

"You have to assume that each visitor coming into the building is an undercover agent investigating the true behaviour of staff."

Likewise, in business you have to develop a mindset to make money. You have to see the opportunities others are not seeing, otherwise you would be there staring blankly as opportunities keep passing by.

Don't call my bluff.

I'm going to seize this moment like a drowning man grasping at a passing branch. I have set my New Year's resolution to do better than I had done last year. I know I can do it. I'm conscious of the waning power likely to conspire against my best intentions. So, the first thing is to put a stop to this negative attitudes.

I read it somewhere and found it interesting to jot it down:

"Read as if you're not going to die."

"Live your life as if you have only one day to live."

A story goes this way. Plato, a student of Socrates wanted to have knowledge and wisdom like his master. So Socrates walked Plato to the ocean and they got into a level that could cover them. Socrates held Plato's head under the water. It was said Plato was gasping for air and was struggling but Socrates could not let him off for certain time. When Plato was lifted, he complained that Socrates was planning to drown him. He replied to Plato: "When you desired my wisdom like you desired that breath of air, only then you can have it." To be successful in business, you need have a business mindset.

Enjoy this powerful mindset from John Legend: "...even when I am losing I am winning."

CHAPTER 3

RESPECT FOR ONESELF

PERSONAL DISCOVERY

Reclaim your territory: The mind
To respect something is find something valuable.

If want to look at anything, there's only one thing I check out for: The EUS(Essential Underlying Spirit) and this gives rise to RESPECT.

You cannot be successful in life without having full control of your mind. This is the secret of success. The is the invisible part of our being. This is the highest power God has given to man. Ninety percent of what one achieves depends on the control one exerts on their mind.

Remember, anyone who is not in full control of their mind is a captive. I know you don't want to be a prisoner, you're gonna kick out the bad guys who occupied your territory and then fence your territory so they don't come back. Keep it under lock and key. Of course, few of the bad guys will question your authority. You have to tell them that you don't need any approval to claim what belongs to you, period! Like I said in the introduction, the root cause of despair and failure in business is in the mind. This is why this book takes 90% of action on discovering self. The greatest conquest in life is that of the mind, therefore this book will lead you through this journey of life. The aircraft is designed and built to fly. All the necessary things fitted and it is up and running. All of it depends on the pilot. Your beginning may seem humble but you have a prosperous future.

No one can change you but yourself.

We need to re-educate ourselves because the education system was programmed to produce graduates who will be employees rather than employers. It is a kind of socially constructed project to limit and control people.

This is what you have to unlearn; anything learnt can be unlearned. Most of the things we learnt have created a huge wall around us that we can't see. Many are crippled and hands tied and cannot make things happen. As a horse is bridled, so are many. This is what kills people's spirit. Birds born in a cage think flying is an illness, this is a result of your environment. This is what springs in the mind of some people. You have to clearly dismantle this wall, brick by brick. Otherwise, you cannot be a transformed person. Once transformed, you cannot return to your old ways. This is where consistency counts. This is where habit counts. This is where discipline counts.

Most people do not recognise the huge power they have; power to change things; power to dominate in their area of influence, power to be successful. You must change that mentality that kept you in ignorance and fear that control you. You must distance yourself from ignorance.

I said, You are 'gods'.
You are all sons of the Most High.
Psalm 82:6

All you require is you and your ability to think things into being. This is why everything in the creative process depends on you. You are a spiritual being living in a physical body.

You can start with nothing, and out of nothing and out of no way, *a way will be made.* **Michael B Beckwith**

GOD has made you. God and you are the greatest because the one inside you is God. This is how powerful you are. Nothing shall remain impossible for you. "Nothing can resist human will," said Benjamin Disraeli.

According to Jesus Christ, you have been given key to the kingdom of God. Whatever you ban on earth is banned in Heaven. Truly God has made you God for His purpose. Muhammed ALI said: "I am the greatest." Many did not understand what he meant. He is literally saying – 'you are the greatest.' God is the greatest and He lives inside you. You are divine—a living, breathing, pulsating particle of God. You are wonderfully made. You are beautiful, complete and lacking nothing. You are created to be successful. To compete is in our blood. You are chosen by God. 'I am', is fundamental. Only by knowing yourself can you become great. Through self knowledge, you develop character and integrity. It helps you to develop culture. The greatest question: "Who are you? Until you know who you are, you are not going anywhere. We see the world not how the world is rather how we are. How you are gives you, your perception.

Life is about converting nature to culture and achieving the best results with a minimum amount of resource.

Nature is for God; culture is human.

God has made nature and left His legacy. In the same vein, we have to create culture that we leave as legacy. Without a powerful culture, there is no sustainability. Culture, in essence, forms environment. This determines how effective we can be. If you don't know who you are, then it becomes difficult to know your vision and purpose.

"Who do men think I am."

You are the son of God.

You are the light of the world as long as you are living on earth.

For you to have RESPECT for yourself, you must first understand who you are. Remember when God said: "I am who I am." This means you must operate only on who you are! YOU must become whom you are. We are who we are, no more no less. This is the origin of authenticity. Never on another person's terms. This leads us to the most important question: "Who are you?" Until we answer this question, one's purpose, mission and vision will never be realised. This is what gives you a powerful head start: a strong sense of mission that is unstoppable, unshakeable belief in yourself. The man who does not understand himself may never master anything. Knowledge of self enables one to control one's emotions, understanding in order to make conscious decision. The first thing God gave to human is the self-image, ie Image of God. The second thing is the presence of God and the third thing is work. Again work to become who we are. These gifts of God then call for RESPECT 'R' hence The big 'R' Of A Successful Business is conceived nurtured and born. This Respect enables one to have habit. This enables your work to be perfect: His image, His presence.

You must understand what Jesus Said: "You either make the tree good and fruit good or You make the tree bad and the fruit bad." The choice is yours.

Therefore, I propose you make the Tree good and the fruit good. Having made that choice, it then means you cannot separate the Tree from the Fruit. One cannot make fruit bad except the fruit makes itself bad. We are children of God and it is impossible to separate us from our Father who is God. No one can separate you from God unless one separates themselves from God. That is why you have respect for yourself.

If you read about Bartimaeus in the Bible, the blind man who had a rare chance: one out of 200 trillion chances of proving who he was; to carry out his vision. The crowd wanted to abort it. The man refused to be silent over an opportunity he's been preparing for from birth. Let me state it clearly: your vision is more important than your life. This vision is your purpose in picture and you clearly have golden opportunity; a rare opportunity to deliver it. You are like, 'one in 200 trillion chances.' Why does one throw away this golden chance in you? Why do you have to sell your birthright like Easu? Proving who you are, and letting this opportunity to slip through your fingers, is a serious concern. What God has left in your hand: your talent to carry out in your lifetime is vital. This gift deserves RESPECT and not to be buried because of what the world will say or friends and family's persuasion. What has external voices got to do with your vision?

Success in life starts in the mind. All our achievements begin in the form of thought: All battle is fought in the mind.

If your mind is conquered, you are going nowhere.

Solomon the wisest man says: "Whatever a man thinketh, so it shall be."
Proverbs 23:7

God created us to be gods and has given to us all things that our minds could picture. There is nothing you really put your mind and heart to that you cannot achieve. I love to take a holistic view of things. That involves engaging and developing the whole person, including conscious and unconscious aspect of the person.

Attached in all this is the self-awareness and values one has for themselves:

I met a friend who said I grew up from day one as Alhijo the great. This is the name my peers call me. This gave me that strong sense of mission early from growing up. It's stored in the subconscious part of my brain. It is in my psyche. What makes us great is when we know who we are and build our talent around that rock. Once you have made up your mind to operate with your talent, the gift of God within you, then you are unstoppable. Without one operating on their talent, you cannot be successful. One only tries to survive and exist and not become significant.

Your ultimate success in business and in life depends on how well you know yourself because we see the world as we are not as they are. Apart from exploiting one's full potential, one knowing themselves give them that authenticity.

We're a bank of gold, a bank of diamond, and a bank of talents. You simply have to convert them to currency. So that you can buy what you like. You are in business. You can now lead a fulfilled life: make a difference!

SELF-WORTH

When I meet people I look at how they worship their God through how they do their work.

First, you have to know your worth! God has already made you unique and great. God has made you God. You are a spiritual being living in a physical body. This is self-awareness! Remember that our values are stored in our talent. You can always enhance your values by honing your talent. Our worth is in our work not in our job. Your work is what defines you. Your job does not define you. You have to develop confidence in yourself and get engaged; go through personal development before you can convert them to currency. This is our pride! This is our worth! Again, the purpose of this book is to help you discover yourself. As soon as you discover yourself, then you discover God and everything becomes possible. This understanding makes you to have respect for your vision. In turn, it makes you form habits. Any knowledge and information that is not acted upon is useless.

When you know your worth, and know your value, then you begin to understand yourself. You begin to respect yourself. Look at your discerning mind.

Psalm:(139:14) says: "We are fearfully and wonderfully made."

You know that nothing can stop you from being successful except yourself. When you have an understanding of yourself, then you have the audacity to take risks. No longer would you be afraid to take risks when it comes to your vision and mission. We are created to be highly successful, **but we must learn how to be successful**. Birds are created to fly, yet they have to learn how to fly.

Lions are created to hunt, yet they have to learn hunting. We are created to be leaders in our own field, yet we have to learn the principles of leadership.

Nobody can set a limit to what you can do and achieve. You are limited by your own thoughts and feelings. It is only your environment that imposes a limit to what you can do. More often than not, we do accept these terms. Remember, your environment includes friends and family members. Again, birds born in a cage think flying is an illness.

You cannot go to God without faith, so you cannot go to business without risk. This single realization is the difference between being a successful entrepreneur and the unsuccessful one. When you have a complete understanding of yourself, then you develop an attitude of fearlessness.

If you don't have respect for yourself, then you have no need for discipline. A person without discipline has no defence for self. It is like one who has no knowledge. Never take discipline for granted.

If one doesn't know oneself, then you won't be able to prioritise your needs. You do not know what wants and needs are in the first place. When you know your purpose and vision, you start getting your priorities right. You begin to see that success is nearer than you originally thought. For you to be successful in business, you have to put the interest of the business above personal interest.

When you have respect for yourself, you start to set realistic goals for yourself because you know yourself. Then comes habit and authenticity. If you don't know who you are, you can't be authentic. It is impossible to have self-expression.

When you know and respect yourself, you will not be content with the less. It is in your DNA to produce more. Why settle for less when there is a huge demand for your talent? Why shrink and kill off your talent? This is pure ignorance and fear. We know our intelligence, courage and ability are rooted in our understanding of who we are.

You should bear in mind that you are the initiator, the one who started the vision before others buy into your passion. You must always monitor what goes on. You must not be complacent. In as much as you trust your lieutenants, you must always check if they are following the rules.

You must always be in touch with your team.

If you do not have **RESPECT** for yourself, then you will always be in the wrong place at the wrong time. Likewise, you will always be the wrong guy. If you do not **RESPECT** yourself, that means you do not know who you are. And the most important question in life is: Who am I? If you do not know who you are, then you cannot have a **RESPECT** for yourself. If you do not have **RESPECT** for yourself, then you do not have a value for yourself. For you to have **RESPECT** for yourself, you must have known who you are. If you do not know yourself, you will never know what you want. If you're asked what you want you would say "a faster horse" as noted by Henry Ford. Respect is never weakness.

When one understands oneself, it leads oneself to see themselves as competent and valuable asset. This moves oneself to another level where one feels confident to handle other things that can affect them in future. **The truth is, the power lies inside you!**

It all starts with the value we have for oneself, of what is important at a particular time and place. It's all about your purpose, mission and vision in life. Understanding these elements will help one resolve the difference between success and failure in business. Once you identify your vision, you start working your way back to one point: **ONESELF.**

If you don't know yourself, then how can you lead yourself? If you can't lead yourself, then how can you lead others?

Lastly, if you understand yourself, then you understand others. **If you put your house together, you also put the world together.**

Look at this story from Breakthrough to peak performance by Jim Steele, Martin Coburn and Colin Hiles.

'A father wanted to keep his young son busy while he got on with some work. He found a complex picture of the world in an old magazine, so he tore it into small pieces and challenged the boy to reassemble it. You might call it a homemade jigsaw puzzle.

Just a short while later, his son came back with the picture completely restored. "How did you manage that so quickly?" his father asked. "It was easy, " said the boy, "There was a picture of a man on the other side of the page. When I put the man together, I had put the world together as well!"'

Start with yourself and the world follows. If you want to change the world change yourself first. Lead by example.

PERSONAL BRANDING

Having understanding of oneself is vital to personal branding. Does one see themselves as a leader? The next step is for one to leverage this understanding through branding of self. Personal Branding is so strategic in business that many business owners are not leaving anything to fate, and not leaving any stone unturned. If you don't keep up to the pace of changing the world of business, then competitors will shovel your brand to the wayside.

Branding is the soul of your business. What is your client/customer's total experience with you and your products and services?

Brands are using social media. They are a huge advertising machine and use PR to sell themselves to the public. To be frank, digital technology has revolutionised things that people who don't take onboard social media are coming home blaming themselves.

The key to Personal branding is integrity. Gamble with honesty, and your brands fly off the shelves as quickly.

Jeff Bezos, founder of Amazon, said: "Your brand is what people say about you when you're not in the room." It's like keeping silent and the impression people have of you will be doing the talking. It is walking the walk. How does one package oneself? In an elevator pitch, what can one say about who they are? What makes you tick? What makes you unique? Your self-worth, like-ability, trustability and knowability. What value does one bring to the market? How does what one do resonate with the people? What messages does one send? What would you like to be known for and what do you stand for?

Personal branding is not only logo, or website or name. It is our personality, image, our products, services and our relationship with our customers. If you are perceived as fake, then your product and services are instantly downgraded. Remember what Michael Shea said in his book, **'Personal Impact:'**

"We are born equal. Quite a few of us got over it by working up our image."

Many are called, yet few are chosen. The art of being chosen involves hard work and transformation. It involves working up our image. The messenger and message must be held in high repute.

This put one's image in the spotlight. London property is built on this principle. The houses are priced high, not that the houses are so fantastic but it's the image which London conjures. Businesses are built on integrity; and, once the integrity drops, then the value plunges.

Truth is the most important thing in branding. Truth is most powerful thing in the universe. Truth is the most fundamental thing. It is the foundation of all things. Integrity is based on the truth. That is why Walter Landor says: " A brand is a promise." Defining your value as something you must do no matter how difficult it may be. Even if it hurts, you will still deliver. The values of products are high because of hype around it. You do hear people say: "Whatever I touch turns sold." Or you see celebrities that are powered by personal branding. This is a result of the picture of these celebrities that consumers have in their mind; it influences them. This is the importance of personal branding. How do you communicate this to your clients? What is it that you do? Can you sum up your messages in 10 words or as in elevator pitch? What is it that makes you unique – the identity that excites and resonates with your audience? What perceptions does your brand communicate? Does it send clear and consistent message that aligns with your mission and vision? Who are you? What do you offer differently from other brand owners? How do you dress as the owner of a business? Can you make a compelling case why customers have to buy from you, rather than your rivals?

Let's look at personal branding in this way. God is our creator and we are his products. Our value, uniqueness and image all depends on God's integrity. Since God is unshakable in terms of integrity and His promise is 100% guaranteed, that makes us priceless and unique. We are highly valued because of God. God is behind us and we are riding on God's laurel of authority. The foundation of humanity is God. I do laugh at people attempting to destroy humanity.

Humanity is impossible to be destroyed by man. Without God we are powerless, ineffective and are cheap. In the same vein, the value of a product depends on the rating of the owner. The owner may be in the background playing God. Only people who have constructive knowledge and insights can know that God is working everyday. Again, some brands are trading high because their owners are behind the scene playing the game. Only through constructive knowledge, or further inquiry, would the Identity of the owners be known. Some brands their owners are not invisible, like Virgin Atlantic and Microsoft. Brands like Nike, Pfizer, Adidas see their owners operating behind the scene. International companies are marketing personal brands more than they market the products and services because Personal branding increases earning potentials not the least that the name behind the brand is A – lister.

For Personal branding to be effective:

1. It must not be seen as smoke and mirrors.
2. You must live up to your words and promises, what you say should be what you do.
3. You must keep the pace, time and value.
4. Putting up a persona may backfire.

5. You must have Respect for oneself, unique, distinct, finding value in what you have.

6. **You must be confident and comfortable in your skin.**

I had a friend Michael who used to work in Nesco. He was proactive and knew his job very well. He became very powerful in his field; their clients/Chevron could not do without him. It happened that another company quoted for the job but Chevron refused the new company. Their reason was that they could only award the contract to the new company if and only if Michael was the project manager. This became a battle. Michael became a huge brand. You know what? Michael was bought over by the new company at recorded huge sum of money, not as a staff but as a consultant. This is how to build up personal branding. Be savvy and passionate in your job. I bet you become unstoppable.

ACTION: To improve your personal branding, start attending conferences, enter leadership roles, and volunteering for speaking engagements. Moreover start blogging and recording training videos.

VALUE SYSTEM AND SELF-AWARENESS

The underlying factor here is talent. When one's value changes, their focus changes as well. Yet, one's talent still remains one's talent. For example, when Christ was picking His apostles, He looked at their talent. He picked James in the field when he was fishing. Fishermen have that tenacity to have patient. When Christ spoke to them, he introduced another value into their life and immediately their focus changed. **Their focus moved from that of catching fish in the river to that of catching men in the world for the kingdom of God.**

Again, Saul later named Paul. He had a talent of going to his limit and passing beyond his limit. He is dealing with the kingdom members beyond another anti-kingdom elements, till his values changed after coming in contact with Christ. After that incident, his focus changed from killing Christians to converting Christians. Tenacity to press to the limit is redirecting his talent to the opposite direction. Talent can be used to do both good and bad. All of it depends on the value system.

Focus is important. What is your focus. What you focus on is what matters. And, what you focus on expands.

Personality is defined as behaviours and responses that are predictable in a person. Personality is the product of nature and nurture. Nature is the genetic package which we inherited from our parents from birth. Nurture is experiences life foisted on us, including our reaction, interpretation and the way they influenced us in our lives.

People have either a good or bad personality. Some people call it split personality. It all depends on your value system. One can switch from a constructive to destructive personality. Saul had a destructive personality before he converted and switched to a constructive personality. This was after he had encounter with Jesus.

Any day one discovers who they are—then his talent, purpose, mission and vision, their focus will change. This is vital. Though we can discover our talent but focus on another person's vision to imitate and impress others, finding yourself in a role that has nothing to do with your vision.

One's ability to use different learning processes includes having skills of introspection is necessary for your success.

1. **Discovery**: understanding oneself with respect to one's experience and ideas.
2. **Reflection**: examining oneself, analysing base on one's experience and knowledge.
3. **Expository teaching**: explaining and describing of ideas and knowledge, formal and informal. For formal, you have programmes and courses where ideas and knowledge are taught. For informal, we have coaching by mates, friends or partners.

SUCCESS

Non-negotiable

Success is a journey. Many will start this journey, but only a few can make it to their destination. For many are called, but few are chosen. Many will start a business but only few will make it to the end. Why not be one of the few who will make it to the finish line. This calls for consistency, discipline, understanding and wisdom. The most important thing is understanding and the ultimate goal is wisdom.

The ultimate goal is to bring ideas into action. The ultimate goal is to bring things to life. The ultimate goal is to make things happen. This is success in action. Carrying out your purpose. This is why we have to Respect oneself, people and products or services.

Remember, we're born to be successful, our future is prosperous, God has put into us that special quality in us to make us successful. We may say it is tiny or small, but we forget when the little seed is planted, grows and becomes a great giant. If you think of a tiny stone thrown into an ocean, it is capable of generating not only a huge ripple effect, but it is has the capacity to cover the whole ocean and can rock the ocean to its bottom. If you want to achieve excellence in big things, you must first develop habit in little matters. This is how powerful and successful we're created to become. This made Dr. Martin Luther King Jr. say: "Everybody can be great because everybody can serve." It's nothing but rendering your own service to the world, regardless of how insignificant one may take it to be. One has to understand that someone is waiting for your message or your work to stimulate or spark off their action. The problem is that we don't have the faith to believe in our God. What is our mindset towards God? What is our attitude towards God. My friend would ask: What is your mindset towards the Giver? Albert Einstein said: "Everybody is a genius." Truly we are all geniuses. You cannot ask a fish to climb a tree. If it does, it can spend the whole of its lifetime thinking itself to be stupid. This is the essence of building on your strengths not on your weaknesses. God does not look at our weaknesses but on our strengths. Hence, we should not look at our individual weaknesses but rather on our strengths. If we look at our weaknesses, you might be forced to say funny things about people; one ends up being funny themselves. We're created to make things happen. We're created to contemplate a bold action and bring it to life. We're created to manifest the glory of God in us. If we are not already doing it, then we should have a rethink and start redirecting our efforts in doing it. Jesus Christ talked of being born again. St. Paul talked of transformation. People talked of change. All depends on the context and the perspective given to it. If you understand what these great people said, then you begin to see how they painted the picture of this wisdom. Unless you understand and appreciate this wisdom, then you cannot be successful. No wonder St. Paul said:

For I am convinced that neither death nor life, neither angels
nor the future, nor any powers, neither height nor depth, nor anything

else in all creation, will be able to separate us from the love of God is in Christ Jesus our Lord. **Romans 8: 38-39**

Until you understand what transformation means, you cannot be successful. Success as journey is only fully realised when one gets to the destination or what the sprinters call finish line. Success is about consistency till the end. The success I am talking about is non-negotiable, and that is why transformation comes before success. Success has to do with purpose. We are all pregnant with a message inside. It is non-negotiable for any pregnant woman not to deliver her baby. Prince Ezem Ihenacho also noted in his book 'Our World In Metaphors': "We are traders in a market, everyone must sell their goods." Our work is to free the gift trapped inside human heart.

Let's look at this aphorism: "Someone was sent to change the political Landscape, he ended up being changed by the political landscape."

The following can be a roadmap for discovering your purpose:
What is it you don't like that is going on in the world?

1. It must touch your heart and mind.
2. It must be for the improvement of mankind
3. You wish something could be done about it.

Once you have the conviction, then that it is the problem you are created to solve. By taking responsibility, a leader is born. Be the change you wish to see. One's strengths and talent and what one loves doing are the biggest indication of where one's purpose and vision lie. According to a powerful mystic poet:

Everyone has been called for some particular work,
and the desire for work has been put in their heart.

I remember the day I started to do video on Facebook and Youtube. The desire was so visible and I had to wake my wife up by 2.00 am to video me as I made the speech. Nothing could have stopped the burning desire. It was like the desire was put in my heart. But I thank God who teaches us in our heart. My internal purpose of the video is not for fame or money. I was deriving joy like a 10 years old doing the painting he loved.

Who teaches us more than the beasts of the field and makes wiser than the birds of the heaven? Job 35: 11

CHAPTER 4

RESPECT FOR PEOPLE

The true currency of business is not money but RESPECT. When we have re-
spect for our relationships, 75% of the problem is knocked off. Respect is a form
of discipline and a vital culture that leads to business success. People like to do
business with people that have respect for them. People love to do business with
people they like; they trust they have Respect for them. One cannot underesti-
mate our deep desire to allow reciprocity to flow like a river. A river flows to A
in the evening, and in the morning it flows to B. A kind of reciprocal behaviour.
As noted by Franklin D Roosevelt:

> **The most important single ingredient in the formula of success**
> **is knowing how to get along with people.**

Look at what Warren Buffett said:

> **In evaluating people, you look for three qualities: integrity, intelligence,**
> **and energy. And if you don't have the first, the other two will kill you.**

In relationship integrity supreme.

Anything that is not for others is meaningless. We get fulfilled when
we love another. All we do originates from and revolves around this law:
'Love thy neighbour.' This is why RESPECT is at heart of all we do. One
of the most fundamental laws of human nature: we reap what we sow. If
you respect people, people will respect you.

You have to respect everyone, not just those you want to impress.

There's a saying: "I will have conversation with you so long as you see me
as one equal to you."

There's always a new ground for two people to have dialogue or conversation. Until people realise this, there is no success. This is a point where

people **Respect** others. This is the point of power, love and sound mind. A zone of honour, favour, reward and wisdom. This is point where humans play the dominant role as God. Placing value upon another person, value of worth and something that needs to be protected. Respecting of others includes, allowing others to have a voice, engaging them, sharing their concerns and recognising their frustrations. Lack of **Respect** is alienating people big time, alienating customers, and employees. This is the reason **RESPECT** is at the heart of all we are learning in this '**The Big 'R' Of A Successful Business.**' We have dealt with Respect of self, without one Respecting self, they cannot Respect another. People are highly influenced by individuals who Respect them. People become inspired by leaders who have Respect for them. Respect instils emotional connection that is vital for individuals to collaborate.

When we Respect and collaborate with others, then the result is formidable.

"One pursues one thousand, two pursue ten thousand."

We must adopt the culture of **Respecting** others if we want to thrive and become highly successful. How we are educated and raised has a huge impact in our lives.

Recalling of Tower of Babel:

Come, let us build ourselves a city and a tower with its top in the heavens...And the Lord said: 'Behold, they are one people, they have all one language, and this is only the beginning of what they will do. And nothing that they propose to do will now be impossible for them.'" **Genesis 11:4-6**

At this point, a serious entrepreneur aims to up his game. Customers and prospective clients love to meet both employees and employers at this brilliant position. Relationships are a two way process. When one person only gives, and the other person only takes, then that relationship is doomed. In all relationships, something is required by both parties. The best way to look at relationships was echoed by JFK: "Ask not what your country can do for you, ask what you can do for your country." When everyone involved begins to seek to give their best, then the result is exponential.

The principle of respect requires that:

"You find greatness when you maximised smallness."

You cannot maximise smallness if you do not appreciate others. You cannot maximise smallness when you do not respect individual differences. Ignorant people don't respect other people's view, they don't appreciate shades of gray. Unwise people see things solely in black and white. Until we learn to see things from others' points of view, then we are doomed. There's a saying that goes like this: "What you sow, is what you reap." If you respect people, then people will respect you.

You've got to appreciate others in order to make constructive use of individual differences. God does not focus on people's weaknesses, but rather He focuses on people's strengths. We, as humans, should only focus on people's strengths. It's only when we focus on our strengths and that of others do we find the true meaning of relationship. Hire people based on their strengths never on their weaknesses. To get the job done, one has to hire the right people. These people must have the right skills. Right people; right skill; right job.

Treat people as you expect them to treat you. This has always been the deal. Interpersonal skills refer to how well you relate to others. There's a saying:

"You'll have more fun and success by focusing on helping other people achieve their goals than you will by focusing on your own goals."

Having respect for others draws you closer to them. And, once people know you respect them, then they tend to gravitate towards you. Having Respect for people and showing them your emotional part can encourage them to be creative and imaginative as you are not making them restrictive.

Having Respect for people puts you in a position to identify and understand their feelings, ideas and situations. Putting yourself in someone's shoes allows you to see the world from their point of view. A kind of anticipating what they require, their needs and wants. Without this Respect, you cannot serve them and you can't get what you want.

Remember the 10 commandments are about honour. From #1 to #4, they talk about honouring God; #5 to #10 commandments talk about honouring people. The only way to be great is to serve people. You can't serve people without respecting them. In fact, if you can honour humans, then you have honoured God. And what is the reward for someone that honours God? All your needs will be provided. If you don't have respect for people, then how can one render service that will increase or enhance human value? If don't have respect for people, how can you design a product that will genuinely improve the lives of people? If you don't have respect and regard for people, then how can you design something that will give people happiness and joy? We should not walk in the dark any more because the light has come. We should learn to Respect and honour people in all we do because people are part of our purpose. People are the most important and greatest asset. Never judge people, because if you judge them, you have no time to love them, rather learn to separate a person from issues or problems. Love the person and deal with issue. When you separate a person and issue or problem, you begin to see God in them, the gift, the talent. This will encourage you to care and deal with the issue. For me, the first thing to see is the person and issue comes second.

Human capital is great; you cannot have great company if you don't have great staff or workforce. Great schools cannot exist if you don't have great teachers. Businesses that don't change their culture will soon see themselves being passed over by more flexible, adaptable, creative, innovative and resolute competitors. There was a situation when Oprah Winfrey went to one of the countries in Europe, and went to a shop to buy something. Then, she was one of the wealthiest women in the world. Upon entering the shop, she was treated in a condescending manner. It forced her to leave the shop. Treating people bad, especially people one doesn't know, could cause one huge loss in business. That was a huge opportunity lost out of sheer ignorance of not respecting people.

According to Dale Carnegie: "The only way to influence someone is to find out what they want, and show them how to get it."

Wise people are able to balance their own needs with needs of other people. Until one starts to see things from others' points of view, they will never be successful. Remember, the only meaningful thing one does is the good done to another. The drive to solve other people's' problems made this book possible. Unwise people only see things in black and white and their self-interest trumps everything they are doing. Intelligent people always choose course of action that works out best for other people. In fact, if you don't serve people, you cannot get what you want on a long run. Strategically, you need people in your business or in your life. You cannot do it alone. Success in life is about who you know. One cannot achieve their goal without that right contact. It is like using axe to cut a tree. One needs to sharpen it if they actual want to cut it smartly. The importance of people as an effective principle cannot be overstressed. This short story from the bible can illustrate the principle of People as well as having a right contact.

One time, the apostles went out to fish. These gentlemen worked through-out the night with little or no success. They were professionals, experienced and hardworking, yet they were not able to catch any fish. But as soon as they struck a right contact (Jesus) and followed the instructions that was given, the dynamics changed. They made a huge catch that they were not able pull the net filled with fishes.

This shows the power of having the right contact. In business, as well as life. It is always a matter of who you know. Until one has the right contact to achieve their goal, it remains elusive. You will remain in your rat race without the right contact. You can see that, as soon as the apostles hook up with the right person, that the result changes. We need the people in our businesses and in our lives. This makes life meaningful. The issue of respect comes into perspective. When you don't respect people, then how can you believe and trust the contact?

Communication is beyond the ability to see another person's side of situ-ation. In involves resolving conflicts, respecting people. Likewise, it involves diversity and the ability to read between the lines. Do you have a genuine concern for others? Are you open to other's ideas? Never let pride and poli-tics in-between your staff.

> *It's our relationship with others that often gives us*
> *the courage to succeed.* **Richard Dale**

You cannot succeed in business without the right people. Remember, as en-trepreneurs, your duty is to make fruits good and not bad. If you are making fruits bad, then you are working against God; you're going to fail. One of the ways to make a fruit bad is to disrespect and dishonour people. You have to respect and honour people—regardless of their age, sex, race and background. God is good. His fruits are good, except individual fruits that chose to make themselves bad.

"Humans must breathe, but corporations must make money." says Alice Embee.

Business is not difficult. It is the people that are difficult. You have to understand the psychology of people.

Appreciate others in order to make constructive use of individual differ-ences. As founder of a company, you need to be able to make people come together around your stated vision, goals and mission; they need to resonate with them. Your vision should be a source of energy and enthusiasm to your staff or employees. **You should be able to exhibit the emotional side of you to inspire everyone to tow the line. It takes humility and courage to lead people around a vision.**

This sense of appeal will motivate them to go extra mile in carrying out their responsibilities without any sense of doubt and uncertainty or ambiguity. You must show that charisma and gravitas appealing to younger talent, in order to retain them in your business. What values, beliefs and image are you projecting? Can you align them with the vision and mission of the company? Are they relevant to our time or are they out-dated and old-fashioned beliefs? Are they values that are dragging the society back to the 15th century? What is the corporate culture? Are they built on individual respect and honesty? Is it a cheating one that had hidden agendas meant to disenfranchise staff and suppliers and customers? As an owner of a business, have you brought in a conducive environment that is healthy enough for your staff to make conscious decisions or to carry out their duty without fear or favour? How far can you trust your staff as to delegate? Do you have a culture of accepting, and promoting inclusiveness and diversity? Do you have Respect for people of different race and gender? Can you spot conscious and unconscious bias existing in your company?

The seed is you. The powerhouse is where everything starts. This is where the seed of respect and discipline will produce the fruit of success in business is sown.

This is why you have to respect another person: I never set to write this book. One day I was writing an article to publish on our magazine website on how to start a business. While I was struggling with the topic, I told my colleague called **Kevin Reddy** *from South Africa that the theme was 'How to be successful in business.' He was inspired, so he instantly gave me 3 points: 3Rs of business. Immediately, I knew that I had been given a powerful seed that needed to be sown. The idea was crystallized and the book* **"Big 'R' Of A Successful Business'** *was written. If I had not had Respect for my colleague, then I would not have intimated him with the difficulty that I had in writing the article in the first place. If I had not respected him, I wouldn't have considered his words. And, I would have taken them for granted. Now, the Respect I had for him had given me instantly and elegantly £1m. This is one of the ways RESPECT can change your life and the world completely. Every entrepreneur should understand this philosophy behind* **The Big R of a successful business.**

As a leader, your job is to establish a clear vision. Formulate a strategy that will make this vision work. Then, both vision and strategy must be communicated to all the members of the staff. People are out for themselves without a shared vision. Everyone pulls in a different direction. No one is an island, but just remember this: what you don't know, another person surely knows it. According to Marcus Aurelius: "If you find something very difficult to achieve yourself, don't imagine it impossible. Anything that is possible and proper for another person can be achieved as easily by you."

Archbishop Desmond Tutu said, "A person is a person through other persons." We need another person to be great.

As a result of your great potential and the capacity, you can produce a brand that can set you apart from other brands. When you have respect for yourself, then you start to see these potentials and capacities within you. You know you are a spiritual being living in a physical body when you have respect for yourself. You have infinite intellectual potential you can tap in to create your world.

Every human has two jobs.

1. an artist
2. a salesperson

Everyone of us is unique in our own way. No two people are the same. Our choices, decisions and experiences in life leave traces on the canvas. These make us so unique and different that they overlap our vision. Your capacity to utilise this experience and maximise it determines your value in the market place. The struggle you are in today is developing the strength you need tomorrow, as the saying goes. Artists always aspire to achieving the best result with a minimum amount of resources. That is why they love simplicity. That personal expression of inner and outer qualities. Michelangelo said that inside every block of stone or marble dwells a beautiful statue; one needs only to remove the excess material to reveal the work of art within. We need to free the gift trapped within us.

As a salesperson, you are the best person to sell yourself. You are the best person to enhance your values. If you don't sell yourself, then nobody will know what you can do and the services which you are capable of rendering. It is not what you know that matters but who you know. It is you that will make yourself relevant in the world. People identify their talent via their strengths; they sell it to the world. You excel in the world by selling your ideas and projecting your authority. Look at John Proctor; he has idea about paradigm and sells it to the world. He has been selling one idea for more than 50 years. At C. Hub Magazine, we have been selling Africa to the world. Projecting Africa in the best possible image.

There is a concept that each person is only six contacts away from any person in the world. This is six degrees of separation. If you want to contact anyone in the world, then it just takes six people to reach that person. All you need is to ask people. Before you know it, you get the person you want to contact. You can work as much as you want, but if you don't have the right contact, then you cannot make a huge difference. What you think is hard is not hard for another person. What you believe to not be possible for you will surprise you when someone else does it. Your talent makes you who you are. Your talent makes you significant. Your talent would be wasted if people who require failure to see, hear and touch it. Your presence is important; you need to be visible and consistent to make a huge impact.

You know when and where to invest to yield utmost result when you have respect for yourself. Time and location is essential. As a unique individual, only you know your purpose and mission. You should focus on that. You have to stay in your gift. You don't see a bird becoming a sheep or dog.

It's seen as a catalyst for their ambition, beliefs or talent. Having RESPECT introduces you to yourself. In turn, have a Respect for others and don't forget that 'Love thy neighbour' is the essence of vision and purpose. The aim of every vision is to improve the lives of others. Respect encourages one to be creative, develop rigour, technique and discipline required to refine your talent. To be the best, it has to come from inside. To be successful, it has to start from inside. We want to be successful in what we do, but we don't want to know what happens within our heart and mind that gave rise to excellent and brilliant works which we see everyday. Sadly, a great number of people are only interested in the success of the business. Yet, they are not interested on how to get there.

Simple talent is never enough. You need to refine and burnish that innate gift. If you have talent, then you need to grow it and refine it. It is a seed. It's about learning to be fairer and not hurting people's feeling.

FUNDAMENTAL PILLARS OF BUSINESS.

Archbishop Desmond Tutu said: "a person is a person through a person."
According to Alice Roosevelt Longworth:

If you haven't got anything nice to say about people, come sit next to me.

Disrespecting people will definitely affect you and will undermine your own power to succeed.

The greatest ability in business is to get along with others and to influence their action. **John Hancock, American politician**

The first step in building rapport is **Respect**. If you don't **Respect** people, then it becomes hard to motivate them.

People love to give their loyalty to leaders who open doors of opportunities for them. Leaders who give their employees full sense of confidence and excitement. A boss that motivates by appealing to their inner desire to excel, challenge and inspire their staff. You cannot look after your staff if you simply don't have **Respect** for them. Such leaders will only be stoking their fears and anxiety, which will on a long run demoralize the staff, kill off their self-confidence and drain off any little courage left with them.

The person you took for granted today may turn out to be the person you need tomorrow. A tree cannot make a forest.

You need people in business, for without people there is no business. Even your critics have something to offer customers. They generate turbulent buzz needed to get your business noticed and they deserve to be respected.

Understanding the needs and desires of people will help you define your products and services to suit and appeal to your customers.

If we go to people with trust and confidence, in return they give us trust and confidence. All businesses need people because people evangelise the products and services. Customers that have never purchased their products and/or services may not have known the producers enough. At this point, everything works for our purpose.It is said that when you are good in what you do, even your competitors become your friends.

With social media, people can easily influence their audience to become loyal to a brand. I have seen people promoting my business without being my client first. Most likely they may have heard about us from their friends who have had experience with my brand.

All businesses are meant for profits; when you add value to your customers and solve their problems, they provide profits. For this sole reason, all businesses focus on customers. I emphasise; all we target is the customer.

Customers, employees, and potential customers are subsets of people and on this basis. We categorise people to define customers, employees and potential customers. The question is:

Do you connect on a human level?

CUSTOMERS

The aim of a business is to satisfy the customer. There is no business without the customer. Customer is the king. Winning the hearts of customers is the most important job.

We should never be allowed to forget that it is the customer who, in the end, determines how many people are employed and what sort of wages companies can afford. **Lord Robens**

The customer is the one who buys your products and services. They are the ones we aim to appeal to in business and they are the ones who keep our businesses going. Our products and services are all we have in the first instance. Do the customers love it?

We express ourselves through our products and services. This is what attracts the customer. This presents us a choice to refine our products and services to keep our customers satisfied. We live in a competitive and changing world where the customers have choices to engage with us or with others as we may not have the monopoly over any products and services. This room for customers to manoeuvre has made it necessary for proper branding and effective marketing.

The competitive nature of the market has made customers not only kings, but the first and last word of a business. To operate on top performance, we've got to package our products and services in a way that no other producer can match. We have to align our products and services with the needs of customers. We've got to be ahead of our competitors in quality, cost and quantity. This bundle includes: good human relationship; effective communication, positive attitudes, beliefs and images.

An organisation must make a conscious decision about which segments of society to serve. Like I said earlier, a product should be able to solve a customer's problem or satisfy a customer's needs.

Our customers are constantly evaluating and assessing our products, services and relationship with what we say and do. Overall, we have to know if we actually know what we are doing. Are we deeply interested in their needs and wants? Are we just scrambling and scratching on the surface?

They want to know if we understand ourselves. If we do, does it lead us to understand them as well? We get all these information through feedback systems in place. If we ignore our customers, to our own detriment and risk – then the business goes down. If we provide them with shoddy products and services, then we lose the plot. We must always be on the side of the customers if we have to win. We have to serve them. Our focus should be on understanding how they want us to serve them at the point of their needs. Our customers are not only buying from us the goods and services, they are buying and sharing our vision through the products and services. That is why we need to **Respect** and appreciate them. They help to evangelize and sell our products and services even when we are not aware.

If you're not enabling your clients, you're disabling them! Rolf Hanusa

During networking, people I engage with love to see what I do when I tell them I'm a publisher. Next, they give me a grin which I interpret as: "Do you have the magazine here with you?" And my reply would be: "Here is the mag," I would say silently as I flash it out. Then, the new friend would say in exhilaration and warmth: "So nice and brilliant." I would hand over the magazine to him and wait for his assessment and evaluation. No doubt at this crucial moment he is forming impression and opinion on the magazine. He is experiencing it for the first time, touching, smelling, tasting seeing it live. He could either be swayed, influenced or his opinions improved as a result of this engagement. There may be things he does like or favour. You, as a seller or producer, has to pay attention to understand to his interests and viewpoints. The vital information you gain could be used to change and improve on your product and services.

Sometimes you might be lucky to meet someone who is versatile on the products and services which you are rendering. This is a golden moment, so seize it and interact. I remember when we first launched our magazine. A couple that was amongst the attendees that briefed I and Faustina about the entertainment industry. They even went as far as directing us to some useful websites where we got vital information about our potential customers.

TARGET AUDIENCE

Do I know my customers?

I was sent only to the lost sheep of the house of Israel. **Matthew 15:24**

Hunters are the best in using target skills: They know how to focus and concentrate. If they have one shot to make, then they go after their prey in clusters. They target one knowing, if they hit one correctly, they are more likely to get others through strayed bullets than targeting none at all resulting in not getting any. The same applies to getting customers. *Knowing your niche is vital because it helps your business to connect with someone rather than making it broad where it does not connect or resonate with anyone.* If you target a particular range of customers, then you're smart. Like C. Hub magazine, it is for African and African descent. The age range is 25-35. So, we focus on these customers rather than making it so broad that people will not connect with the content.

How well do we know our customers?

What are my customer's concerns?

The only way we can be relevant to our time is to be creative.

Every business is aimed at solving problems. It's meant to serve a purpose and needs of the customers, audience and clients. We are meant to go about solving problems. This brings to us a level of influence and success. What service would you want to render to humankind? Of course, the one that touches your heart and mind. For instance, I found out that image is important. Discovering Africans and African descents do not have enough media that project their image; therefore, they were poorly represented by the other media. We saw this gap and chose to fill it. We want to give Africans a voice in global branding.

The primary work of a leader is to open doors of opportunities for your people and the world in general. It's said that if you are not opening doors then you are invariably closing them. I believe that no one can be said to be fully enlightened or successful if there one human who is yet to be liberated. What are your customers' fears and uncertainties and other major concerns relative to your business?

Once you discover a gap in a society, it becomes necessary to fill that with your talent. This is a must-have to be sold to the society. The more you sell it to them, the more your value increases. Already we have a unique talent. The problem is always the value which we add to society. It's you that will make yourself relevant by being the best person to sell your ideas. There are numerous problems. Our society needs more creative and innovative individuals to come up with the solutions. What you have within, your society and generation needs them according to Dr. Myles Munroe.

What is my customer's image?

What does your customer represent? In business, customers are the most important factors. They are your factor X.

Image is everything. What kind of image does your customer have of you? The kind of image my customer wants is that my business is capable of filling their needs? Like the magazine, my customers want their story to be told in way they love it, rather than in a condescending way. Do my customers want to be victims? Do they want to be seen as people who do not have strength and power to determine their destiny and future? You've got to know attitudes of your customers and images that rise to their expectations. There are cars and houses that enhance the image of the owners. When you're inside them, you feel invincible and comfortable. Guys, you're working up your images. Don't laugh!

If I want to produce a product or service, then I have to understand my customer's needs. This is why **Respect** is important. If you don't have respect for people, then it becomes extremely difficult to provide a product or service that will elevate them. This is why self-image is important. It determines how you see people. If you don't have a good self-image, then you can't satisfy customers. People want something that will increase their self-esteem. Would my product increase the confidence or self-worth of my customer's or is it gonna give them poor image and make them look like Mr. Bean?

Some shirts and trousers are designed so badly that they make you look like it was designed by a carpenter. I know carpenters do not design clothes. Some products fail to enhance the image of the customers. They make their situations worse than they were. I remember a painter who, after painting my house, left me with sour taste and irritation. This kind of service makes one to wonder if some people actually know what their customers want. The **Respect** you have for your customers will make them feel special and make it possible to bond with them. Many times you could call your customers by their names and with this personal touch that would force them to lay down their guard for trust, cooperation and smooth transaction.

What are my customer's beliefs?

Your beliefs are meant to make it easy to achieve your values. What do my customers consider as significant in their lives? What is their belief system about health, love and relationships, career, personal development, financial and social aspects of their lives? These go to a large extent to give values to their lives. What most people do not realise is that people are locked inside their own beliefs. If you make no appeal to their self, then they only see you as desperate. They see you as someone not interested in their needs and wants. They may decide to ignore you. When you approach people, their mindset is mostly, what is in there for me? One needs to understand their customer's psychology to be able to pull through it.

What are my customers' values?

What value do we deliver to the customer? How does your talent and strength impact on them? You cannot deliver any value to a customer except to know their values. Are the customers concerned about their reputation or social standing? Who are their competitors in business?

Humans are emotional.

The majority of a human's judgement has to do with emotions, rather than logic. If customers do not get value from products and services, then they do not feel happy. They become disappointed; some feel depressed and empty. They wouldn't like to come near your product or services again. Having a personal touch is crucial. Demonstrating your respect and value to them brings out the bond necessary for a good relationship between the organisation and their customers. Self-interest is a lever that moves customers. If you are able to advance their cause and meet their needs, then their resistance to your products and services dwindle. Think of what you can do for your customers.

Solving a problem is about bringing in the values that are missing in the lives of customers. It could be emotional, physical or even both. Our aim is leaving them better than we found them. Motivations are lost when we disconnect with our values. Knowing the customer's value will help you refine your priorities and appreciate the values you bring to their lives and situations. Everything from our goals, dreams and visions are attempts to fulfill our values. Our values are so important to us that, when we lose them, we become disoriented. Customers want to know why they have to buy from you rather than your competitors. Are your products and services meeting these values? Do you know these values? Knowing them is being smart and enterprising. Nike was able to win people's heart by providing them quality and cosy footwear. Coke provides its customers valuable and refreshing drinks that leave them wanting more. Is it security your customer wants? How do our customers measure success? Do they see themselves as successful people or people that lack confidence that require boosting their self-confidence?

Having known the values the customers want. The next thing is its quantitative value: for example, price and speed of service or qualitative values (design and customer experience.

What are my customers' passion?

What do my customers love? How can I decode their passion? If you know what somebody loves, you then have access to his heart and mind. Selling your products and services becomes easier. Why not devote time to study what your customers love and want. They say a snake could spend eight hours studying its prey, while it takes a second to capture it. If you are able to know a person's passion, then you can define them. A problem defined is a problem solved. If you know a man that loves reading books, then buy a book for him. You've penetrated his heart. Your ability to win and retain one customer is crucial. Remember, a drop of water makes an ocean. There is greatness in maximising smallness. What are my customers' work or the dynamics of what they do?

Look at this story in the Bible: When Saul was converted, the first thing he did was to go to Arabia and Damascus for three years. He was on his own, meditating and focusing on God. He spent three years studying and relating with God. What an amazing choice! We need to study our clients and customers. When we see businesses on the move, active and impressive, we should not be carried away. They have done their homework, and that is the result you're seeing. We only see a snake with prey but fail to see the 8 hours it spent studying its target.

CHANGES

What are the changes going on in the market? How do they affect my customers in relative to the services and products we provide to them? What direction are my customers going, and what is my future in that direction? For instance, social media has come to stay. Most people can now read and access information using their mobile phone and tablets. Is it worth it printing and distributing magazine? How do they look at printed materials? While reasonable numbers of customers prefer to read online, some still want the printed edition. We have to take into consideration the shift in demand and supply of all our products and services. Each day brings changes on how our customers view themselves with regards to our products and services. What is trending now and how can I innovate and influence the future or pioneer the changes coming to our frontiers.

Finding what drives buying decisions and behaviours of customers

Influence strategies: There are small and cost effective approaches one can embark on that produce astonishing results. Humans are social creatures that love to be seen in positive lights and gain approval of others. They restore self-images, especially of people around them. For instance, a single decision to publish a few names of people in attendance of an event on a blast motivated other people who were not interested in the first place. A small change to a letter presented to clients or recipients informing them of large number of citizens who pay their taxes regularly on time reduced the debts owed to HMRC in Britain. According to the book titled, 'The Small Big' written by Steve J. Martin, Noah J. Goldstein and Robert B. Cialdini. This change in a letter made the Inland Revenue to recover £5.6 billion overdue than they had in the previous year.

In as much as people love to be matched and associated with groups, on a flip side grouping could turn people away. For instance, if some group perceive that people on a lower economic ladder are using particular products, then the group that perceived themselves as wealthy people may avoid such products. They associate the products or services as for the less privileged.

You have heard that: "it is not what you say but how you say it." Customers and audiences respond to how we communicate with them. If you want customers to improve their time keeping or efficiency in responding to your message, your persuasion style has got to be different. If there's a perception that customers attend meeting late, obviously a message has to be framed in a way that it focuses on positive side of lateness, rather than the negative side. For instance, asking early comers: "Could you tell us what inspired you to be early for this meeting today?" Focus on positive traits of the early birds. It reflects the concept of looking at the glass half-full or half-empty.

Future lock-in: Having respect and understanding for your customers will help to identify the areas or course of action that will best align with their values. For instance, their choice of charity causes that touch to their heart and mind. If a customer is likely to object to certain commitments based on projects or responsibilities that they have at the moment, then locking in a strategy will help by extending their future commitment to start from 3 months to 6 months or more. You go to some shops (let's say you want to buy computer through contract. They ask you to start paying in 3 months to 6 months time rather than immediately. This alone may persuade you to sign the contract.) Getting you to sign for it is a future lock-in strategy and it will be beneficial to them, given the fact that one could change their mind if no concrete plan is made. Obviously, they know that if you agree to that it pays them and you at the same time.

Live up to your commitment: There's an advert that goes like this: "What we will do is what we say." There is nothing worst than not keeping to your promise. If you know that you cannot keep to it, then you better not promise. Never mislead customers because a good relationship is important: a good relationship is the engine of success. There was a service provider that brought misery to my life when I signed on with them. They promised that they would provide me landline, and an engineer would come to my house to do the connection. Do you know that after signing on with them, no one showed up except the little box they sent to me through the post with instruction on where to connect. After connecting and speaking to their customer service, they promised they would send someone to rectify it. Still, no one showed up. One day, a letter from the company came and I opened it to discover they billed me for an engineer work. I complained, but they promised that something would be done. Nothing was done and the bills kept on coming. Today, whenever I see any proposal from that company, I will cast my eyes to the opposite side. That impression I had with them turned me off. This is how messing around with your customers affects businesses. Certain products do not work, and the sellers are aware yet they prey on people's ignorance but as soon as people realise the trick that will be the end of the journey for that business.

Good Human Relationship: When one disrespects another, then they're being false to oneself; that's misrepresenting oneself. This is why one needs to understand oneself first before they can understand the other.

'To thine own self be true and it must follow, as the night to the day, thou canst not then be false to any man.' **Shakespeare**

You need people as well as the connection in business. You will be robbing yourself of huge opportunities if you do not respect people.

When you respect people, you unlock your fortune—not only by principle of multiplicity, but to strive to produce products that make people feel special and empowered by its craftsmanship and quality.

Sir Anthony Seldon writes in his book on trust: "We lower our defences, thereby increase our vulnerability because greater good is expected to follow." Trust is the basis of cooperation that gives rise to a good relationship. If you go to people with confidence and trust, then you receive confidence and trust in return. Trust is believing in the integrity and fidelity of someone.

If you have an understanding of yourself, your mission and purpose which you know assists you in putting the needs of your business above personal interests.

Never change your originality for the sake of others. You can respect people, but not when their motives and behaviour limit your purpose and vision. Then it is no longer in your best interest to move in their direction. No one can play your role better than you. When someone tries to swindle you or rob you of your money, you don't need to aid or assist them. You should not underestimate people or display any complacency that you might regret. We have the option of doing good or bad. *If we are on the side of good, we should never let the evil part of us manifest or come out. It should be hidden, expelled and locked up under lock and key.*

You are the best judge.

From *The Change Agents' Handbook*:

"You do not have to spend a lot of time and effort on those who strongly resist change. You only have to help and protect those who want to change, so that they are able to succeed.

"Put another way, your job is not to plant the entire forest, row by row – it is to plant clumps of seedlings in hospitable places and to nurture them. As they mature, these trees will spread their seeds, and the forest will eventually cover the fertile land.

'The rocks will, of course, remain barren regardless. This is a logical, effective, and responsible way of using your limited resources. This does not mean that you can afford to ignore the existence of committed and influential opponents of change. You may have to find ways to prevent these individuals from sabotaging the process. However, once you have figured out who cannot be converted, you should not waste more time trying to persuade them.' "

THE CUSTOMER

Good service to the customer is most vital. Winning the hearts of customers, to me, is the company's most important job. This is the heartbeat of business and should never be taken for granted. All we do is to please the customer.

There's a saying in the United States that the customer is king. But in Japan the customer is God. **Tak Kimoto**

The absolute fundamental aim is to make money out of satisfying customers. **Sir John Egan**

We should never be allowed to forget that it is the customer who, in the end, determines how many people are employed and what sort of wages companies can afford. **Lord Robens**

''Better service for the customer is for the good of the public, and this is the true purpose of enterprise.'' – Konosuke Matsushita

Don't treat people like doormats!

Potential customers

These are gold mines that are to be tapped, and one must respect them. They are your future customers. You have not tested them. You have an opportunity to prove to them who you are and sell yourself as who is capable of giving an option. They probably have not heard of or used your products before. They are like the undecided in an election. You know your customers and they know you, but your potential customers may not be aware of your brand. In nature, potentiality is important and it must be exploited. You cannot underestimate their powers; that is why you extend your hand of **Respect** to them. With good faith, you can tap and exploit this advantage. Here, a first impression matters. Once they change their mind, then they are difficult to be convinced. The potential customers are target of all advertisement. No wonder Henry Ford said:

"He that stopped advertising is like one who stopped
his watch thinking he had stopped the time."

People who recruit salespeople know the impact of potential customers. I know of a company when they want to bid for contract, there's nothing they cannot do to win the contract. Sometimes they doorstepped the potential customers – company they are looking forward to winning the contract with.

He who is not against you is with you. Even when people are critical of you, that is why they say our critics are our friends. They help generate the buzz. You need to get our businesses noticed. We need to **Respect** people, whether they are buying from us or not. They may in future change their mind to become our best customers. Some customers may at one point decide to look the other way to try other options out there. Some, once gone, will not come back. Still, some will come back after experimenting and perhaps finding the difference. You will never succeed in business without people.

EMPLOYEES

For your organisation to prosper, you need to have a workforce that is made up of the right people that is flexible, growing and developing. You must be able to retain your great talents. Don't let pride and politics come between you and your staff. Give your staff opportunity, for most of them love to stretch themselves and add more value to the business. Don't constrain their imagination. Let them show what responsibility means to them and others. The one greatest quality of great staff is their ability to work with one another. As an employer, you must truly care for your staff. You must go extra miles to know about their passions and be willing to discuss their family matters. Their physical needs are important, such as: outdoor games and get together parties. Recognise them. Give them awards to recognise the difference. With all this, they feel more involved and probably be willing to support you actively in the vision.

How do you select who works for you?

The first law of leadership demands you select the right people. Get the best and right talent. Get the right people 'on the bus and the wrong people off the bus'. You can have the best vision and best strategy in the world. Yet, if there is nobody to execute it, then it comes to nothing. God has the best things in the world for us but, we are yet to have the best minds to conceive them and put them out for many to see.

1. First, you have to look at someone with integrity—someone who has something to lose. One who is confident and proud of themselves. Without integrity, people can do anything. One has to be honest. Arthur Andersen, one of the biggest names in accounting in the world, and Enron (one of the biggest energy companies) disappeared because of unethical practices because their leaders had no integrity. Never employ anyone without integrity. Being truthful is important in life, as well as in business.

2. Someone who shares the vision and mission of the company. Someone who can go extra miles for what they believe. Find people whose initial motivation is not money but are driven by passion for their vision.

3. Someone who feels and believes in your dreams and benefits from it. No matter how they present themselves, make sure that even if your business is going through a difficult time, they will be able to hang on with you. God asked Gideon to take his men to the stream to check them out.

4. Select someone who has a sense of possibility. Find out what they're afraid of and why.

5. Find out what the person loves, as we're ruled by passion. Find out their responsibilities in their life. Do they like responsibility and challenge?

6. Above all, people who are warm and friendly who think like a child are the best. People who are imaginative.

Remember, the best people produce the best results!

Never ask your staff to do what you cannot do. As an employer, you must lead by example. For you to change people, you must change as well.

According William James:

"The art of being wise is the art of knowing what to overlook."

You must know what to overlook when dealing with people; that is wisdom.

Focus is one directional which is customer bound. Our employees are our partners and should be viewed in that way. They are amongst the geese that lay the golden eggs and should be looked after. What excites and attracts employees most in a workplace is opportunity for growth in terms of their needs and desires. As a leader, you cannot invest time to know your employees on personal and professional level if you have no respect for them. You must genuinely have respect for them first; you mean well for them. You cannot offer them encouragement and guidance when you see them as tools or a cog in a machine to be threatened and forced into doing your job for you. Can you, as a leader, lookout for opportunities that can engender a career advancement for your staff—if you don't have respect for them? As employer, do you go out of your way to know what their passions are? When you hear that one of your staff's mother is in ill do you make out time to visit them?

Look at how Jesus treated his apostles and disciples. He visited their homes without the intent to debase, intrude or to undermine them. Rather, his intention was to motivate and inspire them. You cannot underestimate the power of your employees. The ultimate responsibility of a leader is to make leaders. The best way to achieve this is to respect your employees, but first you must hire and employ people who have talent and skill you love based on your vision. Warren Buffett once said; "in evaluating people, you look for three qualities: integrity, intelligence, and energy. And if you don't have the first, the other two will kill you."

After every assessment and an employee has all qualities in the world but has not got integrity, it is a disaster to hire such a fellow. Integrity is the most important quality to look for. *Don't mix up talent and skills. Go for talent because skills can be taught but talent are not taught.*

Your relationship with your employee is vital. Once you have powerful people who understand the vision and purpose of the organisation, you then have a leverage to make them decision makers. They are the ones to go to customers to pitch your products and services. They need you to delegate some functions. This flexibility is important in the business. This gives them confidence that they are part of the organisation and that their boss trusts them. If you give them the impression that they are not part of the deal, then you are creating a mistrust and ill-feeling. You won't be able to tap into their full potentials. You may think they love you and the organisation, when the fact is that they resent and fear you. You need to have a valuable time with your staff and know how they feel. If you maintain a rigid top down command and control arrangement, then your business will not be successful.

When it comes to opening door for your employee. We had a situation where our fashion editor was encouraged to pursue her passion as a presenter and host by allowing her start with hosting one of our most prestigious events. We spotted her talent when she was writing for C. Hub magazine. We advised her to move to hosting and presenting, since her skill and confidence will match such position.

We did not just put it across to her, but that came after we have checked her background, her interest and her personal experience and her passion. We were so close to her and genuinely wanted her to progress in her area and to contribute to the wellbeing of the company in general. In caring and giving her such opportunity the best-suited for her talent and skills, we are able to retain her loyalty till today. Now she is benefiting, and we are benefiting as she is still working for us.

Respecting your employees include knowing them beyond office work, not that you have to intrude in their personal lives. Rather, know them with clear intention to assist and grow their career and to be for them every step of the way.

We had also different account when we recruited a another staff. It turned out she was not interested in working with us. Not many people love to work in an establishment that has just started and are still navigating their way through the market. We had one seminar and she was the host. She was a very pretty lady; I thought she had some experience because she told me during interview that she had a company that was printing and making cards, but along the way she ran into difficulty and could not go on. She confided in me that she liked my wife, her enthusiasm, zeal and her positive attitude and would love to learn more from her. To my surprise, after the event which was a flop, she began to behave in a strange manner. She was not prompt anymore with her duties, neither was she answering her calls. Her excuse was she travelled and was recovering from a bout of malaria. We accepted her excuses, but she began to be worse and worse till one day we asked her to leave. We had good intentions for her, but she was not prepared to do something to project the interest of the company neither was she keen to talk to us about what she thought was wrong. Sometimes you respect and admire your staff, but you find out they're bent on leaving. What can you do? You cannot stop them.

Most businesses are not successful because their bosses never realise their staff are humans who have wants and desires. We have to respect our employees and they should share with the bosses in the same vision for the business. They are the representatives of the company. They are not ordinary people and should not be treated in that manner.

Sharing the company's vision and mission with employees is absolutely necessary. Without providing them with adequate information or trust, you cannot enjoy their full loyalty. Their full potentials would not be utilized. The most you could have if you are lucky is 50% of their potentials. All these affect the productivity of each individual employee. It is believed that whoever has contact with business, goods and services—whether a customer, potential customer or employees—they can promote or evangelise the business. This goes back to the roots: **Respect** people.

Employers love creative and efficient workforce. People are motivated and dedicated to their duties. They love smart people who can work with less supervision and with elegance. These qualities cannot be delivered if you do not provide them with good environment care, freedom and the peace of mind necessary to produce a good and reliable product and service. If you care for them more than others, then you can't lose them. There should be harmony between the employers and employees.

"The worst mistake a boss can make is not to say, 'well done.'" – John Ashcroft

I emphasise: take responsibility of your staff and respect them so that they become your salespersons.

Do not underestimate them; take them as family members.

Collaboration divides the task and multiple successes.

Companies are where large percentage of the population spend most of their lives. Therefore, a route to personal fulfilment, as well as financial fulfillment, is why workers increasingly want to see their employers taking greater interest in the society.

The answer lies in recruitments. You must make out time and money to recruit the best that will carry along your vision and mission to the logical conclusion. People with the best qualities and who are appreciative of the job, people who love and understand themselves as much as you do.

Remember, you cannot ask people to do things which you cannot do. You must be that person who is planning for people to jump from trees, but be the first to do the jumping. People who will trust you and people who you can trust. To ensure that all staff are motivated in order to make their best contribution.

Recruiting people who understand themselves is vital, given that envious feelings are common amongst staff. Resentment and discontent amongst staff, if it's not managed properly, could damage company's operational performance. Ignorance and fear breeds envy. Good ideas could be ignored if stiff competition exists among employees. To encourage share of ideas, you treat your staff as equitable as possible. Stop competing for promotion and bonuses. People who understand themselves have the tendency to believe in themselves and know that leadership is more of being a servant.

Significance and meaningfulness: Staff will become highly motivated and more productive if they are reminded of the opportunities which the job provides them. These opportunities focus on their personal skills and knowledge development. First, as an employer you have to be friendly, open and trusting. Above all, having respect for them is crucial to keeping them.

Getting things on merit: The most annoying and demoralising thing to employees is people getting ahead of others through being a 'yes man' and sycophantic behaviour. Staff believe that people should be promoted on basis of performance and genuine value to the vision of the organisation. A special connection or relationship with the boss could damage things more than they could improve it. These actions suck out energy from the staff and deliver a wrong message to others: do not bother, for there's a way out of it.

Give Staff Opportunity to make their own choices: Giving employees choices is the way forward. What people signed up to or owning up a commitment is the perfect way. *The principle of consistency states that 'people are most motivated to be consistent with those commitments that they actively make themselves.* Try as much of as possible to encourage or commit to what they've agreed to do. Ask for specific plans that include implementation intentions. Have them state specifically when, where and how they carry out their jobs. Agreeing to yes is not enough. Expand this by allowing them to generate concrete plans on how they will accomplish the goals. This involves them looking into other obligations and responsibilities which they possess.

Having staff means looking after them. At all times you must look after your people and respect them. If you show respect to others, they will show Respect back to you.

A healthier and more mature way of working with your employees is not to threaten them like naughty children. Nor scold them like a bad tenant in the book 'Kalango' where Kalango himself used fear, intimidation and coercion to get his money. Stoking fears and anxiety are bad tactics and a cheap way of working with your staff. Your duty, as a boss, is to motivate and appeal to them in a sensible way. You might succeed short-term, but long-term you will end up being resented and hated. The impact of this silly tactic on your staff performance will be huge. Once they have turned their back on you, you're finished as an entrepreneur.

They are not adversaries. The team you work with is vital; you have to take responsibility for them and treat them as a member of your family.

Motivate and reward them: English proverb: *"There are no bad students, only bad teachers."*
This is very important; if a sheep is made a leader of pack of lions, they will not be successful. But if a lion is made a leader of flock of sheep, they become highly successful. Leadership is the most important thing in the world.

Hire smart people and give them room to do the job. The ability to identify the right person for the right job, and train them to succeed at that very job, makes a perfect meaning. Christensen and Overdorf in their book, 'The Essentials' said: " ...most managers assume that if each person working on a project is well matched to the job, then the organisation in which they work will be, too... To succeed consistently, good managers need to be skilled not just in assessing people but also in assessing the abilities and disabilities of their organisation as a whole."

Your ability to select the right people for the right position is the most important factor for success. You need to be systematic and strategic in approaching a team building challenge.

Learn how to diagnose your situation and create action plans to suit your needs. But the manager must establish a clear vision for the organisation.

Formulate a strategy that not only aligns with that vision, but delivers it. Both vision and strategy must be communicated to the entire staff.

According to Winston Churchill: "It is a serious national evil that, any class of His majesty's subjects should receive less than a living wage in return for their utmost exertion." If you actually have respect for your employees, then you should not pay them peanuts. You should expect them to take their work seriously. Doing that amounts to slavery and cruelty. We actually have respect for our employees and pay them handsomely to motivate them to work harder. One of the ways you can bring incentive to work place is through bonuses; encourage staff training and give them sense of belonging.

The staff stand at the intersection between the firm and customers. They are the mediators. Their knowledge of the products and service is vital to the well-being of the organisation—i.e., being responsive to the needs of the customer. The frontline staff must be given that freedom and support they need. Withholding power from employees is depriving them of the ability to use their expertise, and information they already have to respond to the need of customers with speed.

STAFF STABILITY

The challenge for the company is to ensure that decisions taken by its staff reflect the company's overall vision.

A study by professor John Kotter, of Harvard Business school, in his book: 'Where Do All The Paperclips Go?', found that firms with a strong culture, outperformed others.

A good leader must always value opportunities. They must take it as important as their work, because opportunities are honey for employees. They attract and keep employees the same way success attracts and keeps friends. Employees see opportunity as a way they could grow their skills, achieve their goals and aspirations. For instance, I worked in Cyber Bay ltd. I saw the benefits and opportunities that I would get as a result of it. Working in such prestigious place would provide an enormous experience I need to be gainfully employed in Shell or Mobile in those days. The kind of training I was likely to get at Cyber ltd will help me open my own business. But this kind of thinking cannot be useful for any employee unless it's in line with their personal assignment. The support a founder gives his employees will help them to grow and such growth will benefit both the company and the employee at the short and long run.

The responsibility of a leader is to make another. How do you make another leader except when you give them the opportunity to lead?

I see leadership in this way: When one goes to learn driving with those special driving schools. They test you first to know what level you currently are able to operate. As soon as they discover your strength and weakness, they can evaluate and place you to a level of tutorial that suits you. The next step is to allow you to have a hand at the steering wheel, while they take the passenger seat to allow you to have a test drive. It is important to know that they did not leave you alone, but they made sure they observed as you went through it. I demonstrated this when I was teaching one of my daughters how to ride a bicycle. This is what every company should take and treat their staff with respect.

It is dangerous for a leader to be out of touch with their people's needs and wants. You must endeavour to create a level playing field.

CHAPTER 5

RESPECT FOR PRODUCTS/SERVICES

I don't just sell products to customers, I sell dreams. **Unknown**

Everything is about relationship. Relationship with your products and services is vital; it gives rise to **Respect.** In business, it is what counts. Our creativity is fulfilled when we create.

When you create products you create communities. Businesses can forge much closer relationships with their customers, with social media you get instant feedback making it possible to co-create with customers.

We now have power to engage, connect and create a better future. Power which has never been seen before now has a ripple effect. According to Cesar Hidalgo, the author of 'Why Information Grows,' "Products are magical largely because they augment our capacities. Planes endow us with the ability to fly, ovens with the ability to cook..."

Products can augment our capacities in very beautiful ways that dwarf the usual narratives. This is what is driving new products and it is exciting. We can now build our products around needs, demands, requirements and thoughts.

This is something bigger than you and I; it's not just products or services. This is why we have to put aside self-interest and individual differences to bring ideas to life. We don't just publish C.Hub Magazine. Rather, we sell dreams—something bigger than me and you. This is why we have to **Respect** what we do. Your product or service is part of your purpose and deserves to be **respected**. If you have **Respect** for people, then you will always give them the right products and services. **Respect** creates healthy relationship with people. This is why **Respect** is the currency for business. The **Respect** you have for yourself is not different from the **Respect** you have for others. It is not different from the **Respect** which you have for the products and services that you give to them.

One day we were having an event and we gave out free copies of C.Hub Magazine to people. After the event, as we were packing things to go, Faustina looked across and saw that in one of the bins our magazine had been dropped there. Immediately, she leaped through to the bin. She didn't mind her glamorous dress; she dipped her hand inside the bin and began to pick out the magazines.

Why did she do that? She understood that a product or service is part of your work and deserves to be **Respected**. As you **Respect** a person, so should you **Respect** their work. She felt that her work was not **Respected**. You should not allow anyone to undermine your work in any form.

To Respect something is to find something valuable. That is the discipline we are talking about here.

We need to have **Respect** for our products and services, not only because things have purposes but because they can also define and change the dynamics of the world. Products, apart from endowing us with capacities to do things, provide us access to the practical use of knowledge and understanding. It is a way of connecting with others as we express ourselves through these products. "It is a kind of connecting to the infinite being of which we are part of."

Michelangelo said:

> *"Every block of stone has a statue inside it and it is the task of the sculptor to discover it."*

Products are expressing your freedom and God within you; you can't take it for granted. You must **Respect** it. It allows one the power to change their ideas into a sharable reality.

> *I saw the angel in the marble and carved it until I set him free.*
> **Michelangelo**

If I want to look at anything, then there's only one thing which I recommend you check out: The E.U.S(Essential Underlying Spirit) and this also gives rise to RESPECT.

Sometimes one spends their entire life creating a product not only to satisfy our desire, pleasure or self-indulgence but to appeal to others to see us in positive light.

Everything has purpose. We must **Respect** that purpose in them. When we **Respect** that purpose in them, we begin to understand products beyond self-gain and desire to capitalise the market. We've got to have that belief and **Respect**. Producing high quality products and marketing them does not guarantee success, but that deep **Respect** for what you do.

That purpose makes you who you are, while finding value in what you do. Through your services and products, you can recreate our world. They can make our world a better place. They say the best way to predict the future is to invent it. Through the work of your hand, you can change and predict your future.

Imagine how Steve Jobs changed the way we use mobile phones and how it affects our lives and attitudes. Imagine how Martin Luther Jr's service to mankind changed the lives of millions of people. Imagine the impact of Christ's wisdom on human race. Imagine the services of these individuals: Albert Einstein, Mother Theresa, Nelson Mandela, Angela Macurl, Muhammed Ali, Maya Angelou and a whole lot more.

You see how their products and services connect them with the world. Your products or services should connect with you; then, they should connect with your customers. You must be able to infuse into your products and services your purpose, mission and vision. Your vision and purpose should be reflected in your products and services. Someone who does not know you should be able to look at your products and services and conclude who you are without seeing or meeting you first. If somebody buys your product he's buying your vision.

The qualities, values and creativity you cherish should be found in your products or services. This is what makes your products and services different from others in the market place. When you bring even a similar product, you will see the difference. You see the signature, the hallmark of the manufacturer blinking and pointing an arrow towards purpose and vision of the producers. This signal and mission statement is what resonates with the customers or the clients. This is what customers or clients buy into with businesses. It's like when you buy into someone's passion, you have won their heart and mind. They can't resist your products or services because they have seen integrity, excellence and other endearing qualities in them.

Everything in life hinges on gift.

Remember what JFK said: "Ask not what America can do for you, but ask what you can do for America." What is it you want to bring to the market? What value are you bringing to the market? ARE YOU giving the best of you? Is the quality of your products and services different from that of your competitors?

Don't forget that, 'if you come to the people with trust, people will in return give you trust.' Look at how Steve Jobs gave people the best gift in an iPhone and see how people fall in love with the product. The more people you serve, the more you receive. ***There's a saying: "If you give the world the best of you, the world in turn gives you all that you need."*** – Faustina Anyanwu.

Your products and services should be able to speak for you when you're not in the room. When a customer asks the product: "What is your name? It will reply: "Emeka." Next, can you do it? It will reply without wasting time: "Yes I can." Everything we produce has to demonstrate the WHY. If you don't make this difference, or if you can't demonstrate why, then what you produce is a commodity. You cannot avoid being lumped in with other things as commodities. This is why we respect products and not commodities. Products maintain loyalty, growth and inspiration.

Products and services create an image, one that identifies who you are as an individual. It represents your vision, connects with your purpose and mission in life. Your product has to resonate with you. It has to bond with you in terms of all the values for which you stand.

It should be a mirror work of the owner. They must have all your hallmarks and trademark. Your fingerprints should be traceable in all your products and services. From golden circle, we found that people don't buy what you do or how you do it. What people buy is why do you do it. It's like building and expressing why you do things inside a product. When someone see a product, they see why you do it. They see the difference, the cause and belief inside the product. This kind of thinking makes a product stand out and authentic. It's like breathing life into a product, just the same way God breathed into man. This makes a company to have exponential level of success. People who believe in what you believe are attracted by products which you produce as those beliefs are found inside the product. Since everything has a purpose, it means they deserve that **Respect**; which is finding value in what you do.

The key to any product and service is its distinction. If you cannot show that A is different from B, then there's a cause to worry. We're all unique and different in colours and appearances. This is our strength; God furnished us with unique and different talents. The power of a product is dependent on its uniqueness. Distinction is power. If you cannot show that your product is different from the rest in the market, then you've not started.

Another key is, what is in there for my customers. What quality does the products possess that will attract the customers? You must train yourself to think your way inside the customer's mind. You must produce a product that will resonate with them. But there is no other way to think in that manner if you don't have **Respect** for them.

I love seeing my vision come to life in my products. Our products and brands are reflections of our values, our independence, liberty and authority. All these lie inside us.

They embody the values to which you subscribe. This is why we must understand and have **Respect** for ourselves if we must produce products that are connected with people. For my products or brands to connect with people, they must first connect with me – the producer first. When you produce something that doesn't resonate with you, it's most likely not going to resonate with customers and the people out there.

Does your product connect with people?

The only way to win is to create a clear choice for the consumers. These are what make businesses stand out from the crowd.

The aim is to give your products and services that strong sense of mission that's ingrained in oneself. Like a mother looks at her child straight into the eye and sees that same sparkle. One cannot mistake their products, for that persistent bonding is always there.

Apart from sense of mission, your product and service should have character, truth, honesty integrity.

That physical and behavioural truth is essential if people have to rely on your products and services.

Originality and authenticity are what gives your brands, products and services that integrity. It's a principle on which people can rely. People need someone that gives what they say they have the capacity to give. If they fail to meet with what is stated, then people will see them as something in which they cannot rely. Hence, they are a brand without character. They will avoid you and your services. Companies recall products if they do not meet standards or certain specifications.

Brands, products and services should all communicate this set of values. These values are what attract people to your products.

Delivering products for customers should be at the heart of our products and services.

Respect for your customers means you have to produce top quality products and services.

Look at Nike today; they don't mess around with their customers. They only bring out quality products. They're aware of the dynamics and competitions in the market.

Given the huge competitions in the world today, one cannot afford to produce something that does not express that value and appeal to the customers. This will be a disaster and complete waste of time of resources, which will definitely lead to failure. Aiming to produce a perfect product is critical.

There is a common feeling that cuts across the business owners, employees and customers: passion for the products and services. If this link is missing, you cannot be successful in the business.

Some brands communicate luxury, class and edge as well as contemporary feel. These are fantastic products that are irresistible to customers.

Henry Ford said: "It is not the employer who pays wages; he only handles the money. It is the product that pays the wages." Henry Ford (1863–1947)

Perfect products attract customers and leave our competitors gaping.

Good products and services are the products of our talents. We cannot separate ourselves from them. They are simply the best ways in which we can express ourselves. They are who we are, our thoughts, beliefs and values. Good products and services are necessary if we are to make success in business. A tree is known by its fruits.

Products and services do convey the vision of the producers, that is why there should be good channel of communication between the owners and employees.

You have to deliver a product that sends a message that you care more about your client's goals or your customers than your own needs. Understanding your markets, products, technologies, system and structures including culture and politics is crucial.

It's in the products and services that one expresses that uniqueness. It is our power and everything we got. You must show why your product is different from the packs. Driving your brand is important, as well as essential because that is where we express who we are. This is where we manifest our power, creativity and innovation. This is the point where we distinguish ourselves. This is a point of divergence. A point we give ourselves names and we are proud to answer them. This is why we've got to respect our products and services. If you want to have a good product then you have to have a good raw material to start with. You've got to have the best team to produce the best product. People only connect and trust your product and services when they can feel the real you in your product.

As the Chinese philosopher Laozi observed 2,500 years ago: "A journey of a thousand miles begins with one step."

FEEDBACK

Feedback is essential if you want to achieve perfect, excellent and elegant product. Feedback is like a rear mirror that gives one clues and hints as one navigates. Without feedback, one is walking in the darkness. It is difficult to produce excellent products and services that would resonate with customers.

It's said, "You have to be as perfect as your Father in heaven."

Thomas Edison made 1,000 attempts before he finally developed commercial light bulb. Many people could not have gone through this road. He endured many failures but he did not give up. He never lost sight of his destination. He didn't just make 1,000 attempts; he looked at why he did not get desired result. Each successive attempt lead to feedback, and improved on it. Each corrected attempt brought him closer to the desired result. He was not staring on the experiment blankly, but was working on his failures. This demonstrates the importance of feedback. It is hard to perfect a product without the feedback. Many people ignore feedback. As a result, they don't improve on what they have. Great leaders value mistake making as a natural and necessary part of their personal and professional development as such love feedback.

CHAPTER 6

A SIMPLE WAY TO ACHIEVE YOUR GOALS

If you don't have a goal, how can you score?

Goals help to prioritise and focus your energy. It gives you a clear sense of direction.

Imagine a football in a stadium that has no goals. That means it's aimless; a complete waste of time. My uncle told me that any goal that is easy to reach is not a goal.

The goal becomes easy to attain. You can become what you want to be once you know what that is, as long as you have learnt how to achieve it.

A journey of a thousand miles begins with a single step. Start small but think big.

Taking action is the way to do it!

You must assume control of destiny. You must make conscious decisions to change things you don't like in your present situation.

Goals are important. If you want to send your daughter to university this year, but you don't earn enough money to achieve this goal, then obviously you will not be happy.

S. M. A. R. T.

Specific: It has to be specific and clear. Clarity is important if one has to focus and prioritise.

Measurable: Visible and tangible. It is necessary to set a goal that is measurable. If you can't measure it, then how would one know when they are doing well or not? How would you know when to change strategy or not, when to inject more energy into the project or to reduce the amount of energy going on there?

Achievable: It must be hard to achieve within reach; it requires you stretching yourself.

Realistic: Meaningful and make a difference, logical and relevant or bearing to the main vision.

Time: Should be stated 1 year, months and days.

Your action must be in line with the goals you want to achieve. You should be in line with your beliefs and values. Every word is an action.

ACTION = GOAL = BELIEF = VALUE

Let's say you don't have value for knowledge. Setting a goal for reading a 10 novels for 1 week will be a waste of time. The reason is that value determines the extent of belief and commitment. There will be a conflict opposing forces which l force you to go square one. Goals turns to nightmare due to pressures, compromises and lack of clarity on the purpose.

It is value that determines everything. If you don't have value for money, then how can you set a goal to make 1 million pounds. I bet you would tell yourself why am I stretching myself. Oh! My life is more important than this task. This is why I always ask people to go into the field they have passion for.

Write the goal and value associated with it; the value motivates and influences you to take action.

You can break goals down into specific units. If you have 1 kg of meat, and you want to make it last for two days, then what do you do? You cut it into smaller pieces to make it possible to swallow. No one would like to swallow a big chunk at the same time. The same is true for a project.

For example, If your goal is to build your home in 5 yrs, then the first step is to start putting away some money every month. Each time you set aside this money, you feel happy because you are moving in a positive direction towards achieving your goal.

Whatever you want to achieve in life, you achieve it because you are maximising the smallness. It grows like a mustard seed. This is the secret of the world. Everything ever achieved by humans was done against huge odds but, if you believe it—then you can achieve it. Belief comes before you see it. If you want to see before you believe, good luck. We live by faith, and by faith we achieve against odds. There is no need to read this book if you don't have faith and believe that you can achieve or recover from every situation. For me, whatever I pray and believe I have achieved it. This is my belief and faith.

Do you set a goal for yourself?

It is important you set goals. It is important you raise the bar for yourself. Look at high jumpers, they continuously raise the bar. When they cross one rung, they go for the next. They keep on going increasing the rungs step by step. One step at a time.

What goal have you recently set?

Action is important, as well as self – awareness. This question goes into our thoughts. It brings our attention the need to walk the talk.

Goals involve good planning, time management, organisation, and setting deadlines. What are the contingency measures made in case things don't go as planned?

What goals are you currently engaged in?

Again, this goes further to compel one to bring their awareness, the importance of setting goals and delivering on them. Engagement and getting to the end are important. Awareness is 50 percent the battle.

What have you done to reach the goal?

This includes the plans you've made. For the habit of setting out the previous day actions you wish to take before the commencement of the project. After the day's project, be able to review and analyse how things went. What do you have to prioritise to reach your goal? Resources are scarce; how did you manage them? Are you effectively using the things you have available?

Do you stick to your priorities? How consistent are you? Are you compelled to go after your goals. Include the determination and steadfast adherence to the priorities.

Have you set a goal that you failed to achieve?

Failure has much more to teach us than success and there's no success without failure. When you listen carefully, you will find out what and you ignored that made you not to reach your goal. From there, you will be able identify your weaknesses and recalibrate things to achieve more. How resilient is the person and how does one handle failures and/or losses? Would they bounce back after misadventure? Does one recline in one corner to moan and allow the wait of failure to prevent them from moving forward? How do you take on constructive criticism? These are obviously part of the journey to success.

SECTION B

CHAPTER 7

APPLICATION

Putting your knowledge to work

If I want to look at anything, there's only one thing I check out for: The EUS(Essential Underlying Spirit) and this gives rise to RESPECT.

The Big 'R' Of A Successful Business demonstrates that successful businesses run on a principle of RESPECT. When we Respect, then we are putting into practice the fundamental law of human nature: reap what you sow. Whatever we lack shows that we don't have RESPECT for it. If one does not have wisdom, it means they don't RESPECT wisdom. We talked about knowledge, understanding and now let's discuss how to apply them. You might know everything and have complete understanding of it, but failure to apply wisdom is as dumb as one that does not know it. Wisdom is supreme. This section is the most important.

"As long as you are on earth, you are the light of the world."

There's an adage that says: "You don't know what you have until you lose it." You have God inside you. *And God has made you God.* You should praise and worship God for elevating you to this position. I started a publishing company, not only because of the money, but because of the person I want to become. For I have asked myself this single most important question: "Who am I?"

Until you ask yourself this question, you cannot be an effective leader. I found out that all great humans who effectively changed the world positively asked themselves this question. If you don't know who you are; you won't know where you are going. It is vital you have a clear map of where you are going, otherwise any little challenge on your way can knock you off the course. This is why you must discover your purpose. Once you set your objective, all obstacles must give way. You must stick to your purpose, it is non-negotiable.

"If you expect the world to be fair with you because you are fair, then you're fooling yourself. It's like expecting the lion not to eat you because you didn't eat him." Humans make decisions based on feelings, not on facts and logic. So, be as wise as serpent and as innocent as a dove.

One has essential tasks in life: To serve others, to be a good person and to pursue that occupation he loves. This is where passion originates. No amount of fear, nor worries, can prevent one from pursuing their purpose. No power can stop one from going for this purpose.

You must be delighted over your vision. I know where I want to go and what I want to achieve, I have a clear roadmap. I have everything I need to make it happen. You have talent and you are gifted, chosen by God. Fitted for your purpose. Fitted to compete. Competition is in our DNA. Always remember that having a mission is more fulfilling than having a job.

'Your words must match with your action,
otherwise you have not transformed.'

No one can change you but you only. I love this: "Chick! Chick! Come out of your shell. I've warmed you for long. I've given you enough warmth." Come out of the boat, if you want to walk on the water.

If you visualize yourself of doing something, know that you've got the talent inside you to do it. Make sure you are not acting on a foolish impulse. Discerning power is critical here. They say courage is not enough, that it must be accompanied by wisdom.

In writing my experience, I'm not passing any judgement. Neither am I imposing my own values and opinions. Like I said earlier, the ultimate purpose in life is wisdom. The most important thing is understanding. You can't get wisdom, your ultimate goal, without understanding.

If you ask me: "Why are you in business.?" The short answer: "To inspire people to do what inspires them." I know that when I help others to get their needs and wants, in return, I will automatically get mine. The reason we are in business is not just for money; it's beyond money, it's the wisdom. The purpose is wrapped in our story of life. It's bigger than any sum of individual differences. That is why we have to put aside our differences in order to fulfill it. From this forms the basis of **RESPECT** in the book. Your purpose is greater than your challenge.

This is my passion. This is why I have Respect for the *2Ps – Purpose and Passion = R2P*. These two principles are crucial. Many people contemplate a positive bold action but only a tiny minority bring this action to life. This is all down to one neglecting their purpose in life. One must reflect the light in them. It is non-negotiable. Focusing on your purpose imposes a self-discipline and passion necessary to make things happen.

Here purpose and vision are so important; they form the foundation. Remember what Jesus said: "There are two who build houses, one man builds on the sand, without a foundation, when the storm and flood came the building got swept away. The other fellow digs deep until he finds a rock. On that rock he builds a house which storm and flood could not sweep off. Vision must be built on a solid rock. Vision must be built on God.

"Seek the kingdom of God and everything will follow." I always tell people to fall in love with their God and everything follows. Everything in life follows the same way. Tell me if you have passion for your work. Have you fallen in love with your work? If you fall in love with God, then you definitely will fall in love with people for whom God has created. You will make *Respect* a tapestry and hang it on the door to your heart.

> *My heart melts into the ground, found something true*
> *And everyone's looking round, thinking I'm crazy.*
> *But I don't care what they say*
> *I'm in love with you*
> *They try to pull me away, but they don't know the truth.*
> *Keep bleeding, keep, keep bleeding love.*
> **Leona Lewis**

Once you are in love with your work, keep falling in love with it. This is your story. Your life is your story. Your destiny is to follow your story. Always know that your work is your food. Your work is your purpose. And your purpose is wrapped in your story.

It is said that: "A smart person learns from his mistakes, but a wise one learns from mistakes of others." The secret of success, like I said earlier in the book, lies in making the best of what one has and aligning it effectively to what we want to achieve.

As a leader and entrepreneur, it is better to ask for forgiveness than to ask for permission. C. Hub magazine with a vision to give Africans and African descent a voice in global branding, believes in challerging the status quo. We inspire our people to be great through talent and creativity.

We didn't ask anyone for permission to think and act differently.

Your words must match with your actions. If you believe in something, then you must get to the end of it. Most people will believe in a cause; they won't go right at the end of it. My question is why?

I love 'Bette Midler's lyric.'

> *"From a distance the world looks blue and green,*
> *and snow – capped mountains white.*
> *From a distance the ocean meets the stream,*
> *And the eagle takes to flight.*
> *From a distance there is harmony.*
> *And it echoes through the land.*
> *[...] From a distance we all have enough.*
> *And no one is in need.*
> *There are no guns,*
> *no bombs and no disease,*
> *no hungry mouths to feed.*
> *From a distance we are instruments.*
> *Marching in a common band*
> *Playing songs of hope.*
> *Playing songs of peace.*
> *They are the songs of every man...*
> *God is watching us."*

From a distance you think you get the best product. You're gonna sell it with a smooth touch. But, you will understand that this assumption is wrong.

Even with the best ideas, it's not easily sold to people. It's not enough to have a good idea; something else needs to be done. This misconception needs to be corrected. When you plant a seed, you need to water it. Tend to it by applying fertilizer and pruning it.

It is the same way in business; you need to be resilient and persistent and be able to provide the *'Why'* context. Above all, you need the right contact. Introducing a new product is like coming up with a change, people are going to show resistance. When we started C. Hub Magazine in 2012, there were huge challenges out there. You feature people in the magazine, yet they are too busy with their lives to look at it even when they requested for such features. Sometimes the resistance arrives not only subtle, but pervasive manner that you might be out of business if you don't have roots in God.

Some people out of sheer perversity can't appreciate it, even when it is right. That inspired me to write in the book, 'Kalango' that *"you cannot go into the promised land without passing through the red sea."* You can't be a successful entrepreneur without going through all these challenges. The good thing about these obstacles and hurdles; is that they form formidable backdrops that will provide stability, control and confidence to face the business world. The cross you carry will be used as a threshold to pass over to the other side.

'No cross no crown'

The experience of life you are asking God to remove for you will be a ladder to climb to the top. And you're asking God to move it away for you? This is crazy.

PURPOSE

Listen! Your purpose and personal assignment is more important than what people are saying about you out there. Let's be clever about this. Having a boss is not for me. After working for over twenty years, starting my own company was twitching. To wake up every morning to do what I love is amazing. *I do tell people that the purpose of C. Hub Magazine is bigger than me, bigger than Faustina, and bigger than all people. This is why we have put our differences aside and pursue this vision, purpose and wisdom regardless of any obstacles and challenges. No amount of fear for today and worries of tomorrow can stop one from going after their purpose.*

The first book I consciously had a glance at as a child was given to me by an older friend, Jude. We used to call his father Naira Power. This man was very friendly and humorous. Naira Power lived in Lagos Nigeria with his family and we lived in the village. As a child, we thought the man was capable of doing everything and nothing was impossible for him. We always loved him and his tricks fascinated us a lot. We used to often hang around his house to see what he was up to.

One day, the man pulled a trick on us. Suddenly, his dining table was literally flooded with fresh Naira mint of different denominations. 'This is

unbelievable,' I said, smiling. 'Fresh Naija currency.' The excitement and fun we had remains fresh in my mind. The next day, his son came around clutching a book in his left hand. Out of curiosity, I snatched the book off him. To create fun, I started to read the words out with a grin on my face. The first chapter says: "Be wise as a serpent and innocent as a dove ..." By the time I finished reading this first line, the guy had already taken away the book from me. I did not understand this at a time, but with hindsight the drama was a true revelation of what life is all about. Today that puzzle is having a huge meaning in what I do. ***I love to tell people that stories and drama are full of metaphors.***
  We can learn 7 things here:

1. You must be clever; be as wise as a serpent and innocent as a dove. When you work, work in secret.
2. Nothing is impossible, avoid impossibility. Everything you are looking for is inside you. Visualise yourself of doing something, for you have the talent inside you to do it. ***"The world is moving so fast these days that the man who says it can't be done is generally interrupted by someone doing it" – Elbert Hubbard***
3. Look out for opportunities; it will never come to you. Create the future you love because God has given a beautiful future to humans. It's dazzling in front of you. Appropriate it. Always start small. Starting small allows changes to evolve without those added pressure of too much expectation.
4. Be curious; Curiosity is the key to creativity and talent.
5. Be friendly and warm to others that is the essence of life. You cannot be friends of everyone but you can be friendly with everyone.
6. Be like a child says Jesus Christ. And Albert Einstein said: "Creativity is intelligence having fun."
7. Understand what time means. What day means and what night means. What is the opportune time? Or time of your visitation.
8. Freedom time is the fighting,when you start business; the time of responsibility and accountability.

Your success in life depends on your ability to maximise your talent. Danny White said: "*Whatever I have achieved in my life, I have responded to each achievement by aiming even higher.*"

Ask yourself why is it that less than 1% of the world population employs 99% of others. When my friend John told his classmate at secondary school what business he was doing. "Are you joking me," was his friend's reply. So are you joking me! Business needs to be an absolute commitment, passion and self-will and faith. All I have, All I am, and I do, I give it to you Lord. This is the time to offer to your God your gift. Your vision is God inside of you. Make sure you had a look at Attitude in Section A. This is why the majority of people will run away after the first two years of starting a business. In the book Kalango, the first quotation you see reads: *"Nothing in life can prepare you enough for the things you could see."* Unknown.

It's beyond what you learnt at school. It is about how you can think outside the box, being creative because you are going to face a different scenario which is not written in the textbook:

Read:

The sad truth about peacetime rank manoeuvres was that the officers who shone more brightly were those who played by the book. There was no place for individual brilliance or initiative, largely because we were expecting and training for a short, sharp nuclear war.
My training methods were not, so far as I knew, present in any military textbook. They stemmed from common sense reactions to the emergency situations likely to occur in Dhofar. **Beyond Believe**

Starting a business is a great way of taking control of your future. And it is important for a number of reasons.

1. It brings in joy and happiness. Don't forget the main purpose of business is to make a person's life better.
2. It opens doors of opportunities for your people. In Benjamin Disraeli's words: "Opportunity is more powerful than even conquerors and prophets."
3. It gives you a huge insight that money cannot buy. It brings value.
4. It puts money in your bank account. Thereby, it gives you financial independence which many desperately need.
5. You start to see the Lord in the land of the living because the kingdom of God starts from the earth. We see the glory here. You experience God inside you.

Why not inspire people to do what inspires them? This is where understanding plays a huge role.

An entrepreneur must be clever and willing to take risk that, with faith all their heart desires will be accomplished.

There is little or nothing you can accomplish on earth without faith. There are lots of things that happen around us which we cannot see, yet they are persistent. It is through faith one gains knowledge of those things. For instance, our body is in constant vibration. Humans should not be like fish. Fish has no awareness of the water it swims in.

Again, you've got to remember that the crazy ones are the ones that bring changes to the world, according to Steve Jobs.

"Doing the same thing and expecting a different result is insanity." said Albert Einstein.

When we started our magazine with no money and no experience, people thought we were absolutely crazy. This, alone, could justify why 99% of our friends and family members snubbed us. But you have to be crazy to continue doing what you are doing when great supports from families and friends are cut off. This is a delicate time, but if you focus on wisdom, only God can turn you from being crazy to being wise.

Another thing you cannot afford to miss is pace and timing. You may not have any skills, have no money but timing needs to be correct. I called timing wisdom. If you joke with this, then you're a goner. Perfect timing made Barack Obama the president of the United States and Sadiq Khan the London Mayor. Bad timing, of course, is bad across the board.

The test of the pudding is in the eating: now is the time to apply this concept of Respect for oneself, people, product or service to make it happen. One wouldn't hesitate to tell you that faith is the bedrock of everything in the universe. For without faith, you have little or nothing to achieve. It is with faith and hard work that I overcome all the odds I mentioned in this book. It is based on this experience that I am able to inspire you to be great as well.

Everything ever built by man was all done against the odds.
Gordon Brown

In section A, I mentioned faith as Abraham because I know the importance of faith. Not being successful is comparable to building an aircraft that never took off. We all are created to be successful.

Our problems are manmade; therefore, they can be solved by man. According to JFK, as I have explained on the background.

As an iconic leader, Albert Einstein might say that one will never solve problems by applying the same way of thinking that caused them in the first place. You need to move or jump to a different platform if you must solve the problem. The mindset you used in creating a problem cannot be the same mindset you use in solving it. You must change the way you think. You must concentrate your mind on internal things more than the external. It is a fight in a dog not the size of a dog. All things become achieved in the mind before you can see them in the physical.

All problems were as a result of human action and therefore can always be solved by human.

The first point to start with is your thinking. CHANGE YOUR THINKING. This is what St Paul means by 'daily renewal of the mind'. Without changing the way you think about things, you cannot be transformed. You must move away from that platform to another in other to bring a positive change. Move! Move! Move!

Everybody can be great because everybody can serve, said by Martin Luther king jr.

Think of the least thing one can do. Sow that little seed and you become great.

Linking greatness with service

JFK said: "Think of what to do for America and not what America will do for you."

This, again, is service: For me, what hinders some people from achieving greatness is this: The enemy called pride.

Until you understand the meaning of what Jesus Christ, the greatest Teacher said, you wouldn't have happiness, joy and wealth to its fullest: He says: "To be the leader, you must first be the servant."

My thinking changed when I understood this greatest paradox. Remember that when you discover yourself, you discover God and everything becomes possible.

The most important thing is understanding. This is what makes things happen. It's counter-productive to look down on people. Pride is distraction and it is the greatest obstacle to human progress and achievement. Just like all our organs are interconnected, so are all humans. This book wouldn't have been written if I had looked down on **Kevin Ready**, nor would I have made the money I've made from this book. More people wouldn't have been enlightened. I have freed millions from despair and penury. This brings us back to the concept of **RESPECT** on which all principles in business success revolve.

Until you make conscious decision to have **Respect** for yourself, others, your products and services, you cannot effectively carry out your plans, goals and vision and be fully happy and successful.

It's service that makes us great. What service are you willing to bring to the market? What value do you think you can bring into people's lives? What problems are you capable of solving?

Life's a journey! Two most important things you need: Purpose and Destination(vision), where you are going. People perish for lack of vision.

You can launch yourself from anywhere, regardless of your present situation or physical environment. You can overcome any amount of obstacle which is presented before you. My background is God.

If you can't Respect anyone, then you can't serve. If you can't serve, then you have no opportunity of using your talent. If you don't use your talent, then you have done yourself more harm.

The purpose of doing business is to serve. As noted by Richard Branson: "A business is simply an idea to make other people's lives better."

Think of what service you can render to mankind and build your vision around it.

This is where the joy and fulfilment of purpose and vision come from. Through service, you recreate a future flowing with milk and honey. The product you create today, can define and change the dynamics of the world tomorrow.

Pushing the ball into the air with resolve and passion

Never before has mankind had a powerful opportunity to create a befitting future where they can control their destiny and fate than now. We have access to knowledge more than our predecessors. Internet and social media has changed our culture and habit. With this power, we can always realise our aspirations and vision if we show passion, wisdom and understanding in all we do.

I love business that makes the lives of people better, helps one to open doors of opportunity for himself and his people and this is the LOVE which Jesus said is the highest.

And in the word of Benjamin Disraeli: "Opportunity is more powerful even than conquerors and prophets."

The world has changed. So that small businesses can flourish in any field such as publishing, where I am operating. Access to internet and search engines and social media allow our customers to reach us and interact with us. We are no longer invisible as small businesses used to be two decades ago. Now, large and small businesses can connect with customers and potential customers. This leverage is a huge power given to everyone to succeed. It is now a matter of making it happen.

In the beginning, the spirit of God hovered. He said: "Let there be light'
Action now supersedes everything.

All successful people know *2 + 2 can equal to any number you want it to be'*.

That is why, if you do not manifest the glory of God within you, you will hardly achieve a lasting joy and happiness.

You can launch yourself from any angle in life. It all depends on the talent, passion and knowledge available to you and your vision. You can achieve great height regardless of your social statues.

Mistakes, small and big, often provide the best learning opportunities. This knowledge found me asking myself: "If I was not afraid, then what would I do?" What would I love to do? Once I answered these questions, my confidence level rose and my self-doubt varnished.

"The art of being wise is the art of knowing what to overlook."
William James

We start to live only when we are no longer afraid. If you don't risk anything, then you risk more. Nothing worth having ever comes easy.

Here comes the sun:

Business is good, apart from personal gratification, what you produce or do, your generation needs it.

***If somebody offers you an amazing opportunity, but you are not sure you can do it, say yes – then learn how to do it later.* Richard Branson**

Your background is that of God: your image is that of God. All the power in the universe is within you; it means that nothing is impossible. Once you're able to understand this, then you no longer join people who are in the habit of blaming others for their circumstances. Your mindset will change; you will have a positive mindset of '**I can**' in your life.

I am not made or unmade by the things which happen to me but my reactions to them. **St John Of The Cross**

What's the plan for achieving this vision:

Guilt and resentment will phase away. Good health and success begin to flourish with this new environment.

Two things are important:

You must be on the right track and you must be moving.

If one notices a gap in people's needs, then they must move boldly to fill in the gap. This is the way to initiate a product. It is not the customers that tell you what they need, but it is you. Visionaries lead the way. They invent a future and sell it to the people. They make our world a better place. That reminds me of what Abraham Lincoln said: "The best way to predict the future is to invent it." This is how most innovative and successful products are launched. We saw a gap in media industry as Africans do not have enough positive representation. We dug in our feet to start C. Hub magazine. As a rule of thumb, it takes 10 years to build a brand. We look forward to the day Africans will be competing effectively on an international level.

Similarly, Sony Walkman (conceived by Akio Morita) noticed that young people loved listening to music all the time. He invented what we knew as walkman to meet this need.

Sony's visionary leader, Aliko Morita, said: "Our plan is to lead the public, rather than ask them what products they want. The public does not know what is possible, but we do."

Steve Jobs said: "It is not the duty of customers to know what they want."

Henry ford said: "If I'd asked my customers what they wanted, they'd have said a faster horse."

These are what change the rules of the game.

1. Be yourself

Stay in touch with your own values and your own passion.
I've always felt I'm different; that God has given me talent. You have to accomplish your vision for your personal assignment. I can't continue to wallow in ignorance, digest and absorb all the crazy things my environment throws at me. Our culture has trained us to suppress our feelings and trained us to submit. They put a brittle over our mouth that will cause us pain if we do things differently; meanwhile, our power lies in doing things differently. I can't be a child forever doing childish things, for one needs to grow up and face responsibilities. You must actualise your vision, while making a difference. You have to be bold and brave to move away from your comfort zone.

Leibes said: "I would walk 20 miles with my enemy, if I have something to learn from them." If moving away from my comfort zone can make my life better, then I would move. I would take a calculated risk if that would bring a positive result in my life (and the life of others).

You can't achieve this until you move away from your environment.. You have to be confident if one has to show leadership. The ultimate challenge is one being able to conquer themselves.

"*Whenever you find yourself on the side of majority, it is time to pause and reflect.*"

One of the purposes of this book is to persuade you. And make sure you're aware of why you should move away from the crowd. If you want to be successful, then you must follow your own script—not the one handed to you by the society. You cannot be on the side of the crowd and still be yourself. Being yourself means you're automatically successful. People follow the crowd just to see oneself in a positive light.

There are two types of people: Those who look at accomplishments of others and ask: why not me? Why are things working for John? If I buy this book written by John, I'm literally enriching him and making myself poorer. As a result, I won't buy the book, regardless of the content. They see the world as a zero-sum game, where one person wins and another loses. This is not a good way to look at things.

The second person sees the world as a 'Win-Win' situation. They do not see the world as a zero-sum game. They see the success of others as inspiration. They have the mindset of, 'If he can do it, then why can't I?'

We're worried of the consequences of what others might think of us. We want to gain the approval of others, and to affiliate with people. This is a choice you have to make from the beginning. Stepping outside your comfort zone. Your comfort zone is the crowd you are following. You're hiding in the crowd and not carrying out your vision, purpose and mission in life. What values are you bringing into the market and in the world? By stepping outside your comfort zone, you face challenges with sense of urgency, security in yourself and enthusiasm. You enter action with boldness.

2. A problem defined is a problem solved

I want to be different, but different in what? This is the most dreaded question. This is the battle I faced everyday of my life before now. I found that I'm gifted, but gifted in what? As you start to question yourself, awareness, clarity, and concentration become key players. Remember that what you focus on expands. As you continue to stutter and flutter around these thoughts and feelings, hopefully thoughts you had not given attention earlier will start to unravel. They begin to circulate in your mind, releasing powerful and brilliant ideas. Ideas you must translate to actions.

Whatever a mind conceives, it has the capacity to actualise. Ideas are building blocks. Step-by-step you construct the edifice, the cathedral that can house your community and the world. In what way would you like to change the world? You have to always leave a place better than you find it. What will be your legacy? What would you like people to remember you for when you're gone? The universe is ruled and controlled by positive energy. Look at how Steve Jobs and Nelson Mandela impacted lives. How Facebook founder, Mark Zuckerberg, made it possible for us to see and communicate with one another. This looked nearly impossible two decades ago. How Nelson Mandela upturned apartheid that was once a scourge on humanity to impact on all living soul. How Steve Jobs changed the landscape of mobile technology to something never seen in our time. Bring information, shoppings and other services not only to our doorsteps but into our heart and mind.

3. Heart and Mind

What is it that one loves? What is your passion? What brings joy and happiness to your mind? What motivates someone? Is it reading a novel? Is it design? Music? Dancing and acting? Is it football? Basketball? Don't forget that your heart and mind somehow know what you will become. The thought of a righteous mind is accurate, more reliable than science and statistics. You must learn to believe in yourself. Trust your instinct and subconscious.

For me, I love reading and writing. This is where my heart and mind is. I studied engineering, but finally found myself in writing and publishing. This is how life could turn out to be. For instance, Faustina (my wife) studied nursing but found herself in media and publishing.

What is your hobby? You can turn it into a career, something can give you money and at the same time give you joy and happiness. This is probably something you have started from childhood and has been very manifesting as you progress to teenage and adulthood.

Passion is the key here. What are you excited about? Passion is stronger than death. Your passion is your food. A passionate man never gives up. Passion is like talent that makes you who you are. Passion makes you unique and different. Where does your passion lie? Passion spins the plot. When I discovered my passion, life became easy. I know I will do whatever it takes to accomplish my mission. Passion to excel, challenge and inspire.

It's foolish not becoming an expert at your passion. **Richard Branson**

If you have discovered where your passion lies, then you can now proceed back to level 2. Defining your problem means it is solved according to Albert Einstein.

Let's say when I found out what I love. I love reading books and magazines. If I go to level two, then I defined myself as a publisher. So what is it that you love? Whatever you love to do, move it to level two to be able to define it. This is a platform for defining yourself.

Once you have finished at level two, then you can proceed to level one. Level one is what I called '**Assignment zone**.' This is where your purpose is identified and laid to bay. Then, match and mirror it against what that small voice in you always tells you. Don't ignore that inner feeling, the one that you have had since childhood. That is where your talent is rooted. It's what you have always wanted to be. For a believer, that which always springs up when you are praying and meditating. As soon as you measured it in your heart and mind, then this is your vision, your purpose and your assignment in life. When I discovered my vision, I hit the ground running. I have a strong sense of mission.

ACTION: MAKE IT HAPPEN

Start small but think big. "Remember a journey of a thousand mile begins with a single step."

A tree is hidden inside a seed. Every powerful thing began small. Ideas start small and blossom and became powerful.

Taking action is the master key

Now that you have discovered your purpose, vision and personal assignment, you're marked for success. You are now focused, for there is clarity. Your sight is neither foggy nor clouded. You now have area of concentration. When I discovered what to do: To publish C.Hub magazine, I knew instantly that I have conquered my fear. Fear of failing is a thing of the past. Complacency is no longer my home. This is where I can express myself, not only in words but also in deed. This is where my success comes from. My self-fulfilling beliefs are here to stay. No one holds a plough that looks back is worth a salt. Again, the ultimate challenge is conquering oneself. Success does not strive in self-doubt. *Show me a person who has faith without work and I will show you a person who is doomed.*

When you lie in a warm bath, you won't notice a warmth after a while; you can only feel warmth again when you move around. Stirring the water makes you to experience warmth. In the same way, action makes you to experience result.

Remember the stone that the builders rejected. One of the things that inspired me to start my own business was this: I looked at myself. I was already down, had no money, and was living from hand to mouth. I simply had nothing to lose if I started doing my thing. You are already struggling at the bottom. If you fail, then you are already at the bottom. What meaning does it make? Who cares? People are busy doing their things and I was here whinging and complaining when I can do something to help myself. When you are unknown, there is nothing to distract you. No public image to protect and manage, no money is at stake. Tell me why I have to worry about what people think and feel about me; that will stop me from carrying out my purpose and assignment in this limited time I have on earth.

We are all told to come and change things, only to allow the political landscape to change us. Some are melted and dissolved like salt in the background and cannot make a difference. This very thinking inspired me to take action. I have my vision and talent to do whatever God has directed me to do without fear or favour, without apology because they are not criminal nor evil. Each morning I see the picture and message He has placed in my mind and heart. The only gap between me and my vision is that faith in believing what God has shown me. **Always bring the picture up!**

HABITS

A strong man runs his course with joy. **Psalm 19**

What one continuously does defines him, your daily routine defines you. You become what you always do. Everything works on principle and, if one wants something and one did not get it, then it means he does not know the principle. The principle of habit is one of the most effective ways to hone and perfect your talent.

Nothing is stronger than habit. **Ovid**

Don't forget consistency. If one is consistent then they will realise their goal. Consistency makes you to get to the end. I set my goal and develop habits around it.

The sun teaches us that everything completes its circle, and so do I.

In a day, I write down all I want to achieve. I stick to it and make sure I run my course with joy. At the end of the day I say: "Sufficient unto the day is the evil thereof?" In so doing, I complete my course in a year with joy.

The law of intentions

"Whatever you put your attention to increases. My vision delights and gives me joy; that near-obsession gives me sense of direction and passion.

This is how powerful habits can be. "We are what we repeatedly do,"
according to Aristotle. As soon as one commits oneself, providence moves
in. Remember the saying, "When you pray, pray in secret."
I hated this saying, but when I understood it, my perception changed. "If
you can fake sincerity, you can fake anything."
Lawrence Oliver

Creative people do fake it till they make it. Look at children; they learn things by faking things. They pretend to be playing a role until they perfect it. The same way are creative people. They keep practising in secret till they perfect it and when you see them, you marvel. Nothing is impossible. If you start doing something, and you are committed to it, soon it becomes habit. That means it is now in subconscious, you have achieved it.

Recalling Albert Einstein's saying, "Creativity is intelligence having fun." Free yourself.

Austin Kleon, in his book, "Steal Like An Artist." he said:

1. Pretend to be something you're not until you are – fake it until you're successful, until everybody sees you the way you want them to; or
2. Pretend to be making something until you actually make something.

Shakespeare wrote:

> *"All the world's a stage,*
> *And all the men and women merely players:*
> *They have their exits and their entrances;*
> *And one man in his time plays many part."*

Whatever you want to be, start acting it out. Start doing it, and before long you would have achieved it. God has given us a powerful mind to re-create our world the way we want it, in order to suit our interest. Yet, many people are not aware of this power and, therefore, don't use it. Our mind does not recognise what is real and unreal. When a set of sportsmen were asked to run round a field with instruments to record some signals. According to records, certain signals were received and noted. After a time, the same sportsmen were asked to stay indoors and pretend to be running the same sprints and the same instrument attached. The surprise of many, the same signals picked when the sportsmen were running physically on the field tend to tally with the result got virtually.

That means we recreate mentally things we want in our physical world. First start by conceiving it and then affirming it.

Belinda Parmar in her book titled, "The Empathy Era" wrote:

"Paul Zak is a Neuro-Economist and Professor at Claremount Graduate in Southern California. He was the first to identify the role of the hormone oxytocin in mediating trusting behaviours between strangers, and has written on the role the hormone plays in empathy. When I asked him whether the interactions we had over the internet had the same effect on our hormonal response as those we had in person, he told me that although it is less pronounced, the same reaction still occurs."

PREPARATION

"There are no secrets to success: Don't waste time looking for them. Success is the result of preparation, hard work, learning from failure, loyalty to those for whom you work, and persistence."

Having been following me through this journey, it's time you began to think of yourself as a successful businessman. You need to identify less with fear and self-doubt and more with your passion, talent and confidence. Beneath all veneer of success, there is the willpower for one to be disciplined and make necessary preparation with intention to excel, challenge ourselves, inspire ourselves and others.

Remember the saying: "Hard work beats talent when talent fails to work hard."

Entertainment like any other industry is constantly on the look out for the next best thing. The market is highly competitive. God said his message is new every morning and St. Paul talked about renewing your mind. You've got to update your knowledge all the time, as this knowledge is what affects how we see things. We need to keep our eyes on the ball. I'm a bit laid-back when it comes to being professional; it means I need to wake up. Look straight ahead, and give it my best.

I love the Red Cross motto: **"Be prepared." Work all the time, that is what it means to be free.**

You can't underestimate the importance of preparation. Preparation is the evidence of faith. All important journeys in life depend on preparation. Zain Asher in one of her Tedx presentations talked about preparation. She said when they were kids her brother, Chiwetelu Ejiofor, had already started preparing for a role in acting. Imagine at the age of 7 he had already started miming in front of the mirror. For him, he had seen his future and started preparing for something that will finally be fulfilled at age 30. The seed in its smallness sees its future. Its future is prosperous. The same is Joseph in the bible. He saw his future while he was still young.

Our future is in our hands. Once we see it, without a doubt we have to start preparing for the day that it will be fulfilled. It will definitely come. How tragic it will be for us to find ourselves unprepared for that for which is our assignment.

The question I continuously ask myself is: what is the goal for which you aim?

TAKING RISKS

Business, like any other thing in life, involves risk taking. There is no guarantees in business. If it were guaranteed, then it won't be an adventure—but we can reduce the risk. No one is suggesting that you should be reckless or foolhardy, but say yes I can. Even if it means volunteering to do something. The good thing here is that you have a purpose; you have your personal assignment. It's not like everything is coming from the blues. Your mission is defined. The question is not risky, but rather—how much risk can you take at a time?

My advice here is this: take risks based on the ones which you trust. Wisdom and discernment is critical. You have to break down the risk. See it like a Chunk of meat to eat. What do you do? You simply cut it into bits before you swallow it. I know you cannot put a kilogram of meat into your mouth at once, so is risk taking in business. So far, everything is going to plan. The future always belong to the fearless. If you don't push boundaries and challenge status quo, then there's no future. If you stay in your comfort zone, there's no future. Everything is risky. Most times we are either so comfortable in our cocoon, doing things over and over or too afraid to change things; doing things differently.

I want you to be aware of this: When an opportunity is given to you, grab it—even though you don't know it. Find someone who knows it, for this is risk taking. God has given us opportunity in this world, grab it. Start doing it. This is how the world operates. Look the story of prodigal son. When the prodigal son returned, the father killed the biggest ram. The first son was not happy, but the father told him that everything I got was yours and all the time you were with me you did not take any ram and neither did I stop you, you had all the power to pick any ram and slaughter, you simply don't need any permission because everything was yours.

It tells us that God has given us all opportunity. It is left for us to identify what one wants to do and do it. Otherwise, you will be waiting forever.

BELIEF

It is said: Believe in yourself and everything becomes possible. I have that unshakeable belief in myself that I'm capable of doing anything of which I set my mind. Maybe I got this strong belief because of my experiences in life. I know that whatever I set my mind to that I am capable of achieving. Nothing can resist the will of man. Your purpose in life is the will of God; He left in your mind His will. You're God because God has made you God. One of the qualities I have is this: I finish whatever I start. I am that persistent and resilient. This makes me think things through before I start. There were several ideas we had and I discarded them. Not that we couldn't make them happen, but I simply didn't have the interest that will last me to the end with such projects.

Naturally I believe I have energy and would like to drop it on something meaningful. When Faustina came with the idea of the magazine, I was excited. My enthusiasm was high and I did not waste time to carry it onboard, despite the fact that none of us had any background in journalism. The idea chimes and resonates with my inner spirit. I knew from day one that we would succeed. We can do whatever it takes. For me, I have had much difficult encounters in my life and I succeeded. My experience at university prepared me physically and emotionally for anything that would come on my way. As a voracious reader, I know I may have read stories that showed how formidable human spirit is. I read on the newspaper where it was stated that former Chelsea manager Jose Mourinho said: "Human will is stronger that nuclear atomic bomb. That this is not his words but the word of Albert Einstein. You cannot maximise the power and knowledge of which you gained in this book without having faith. Faith is the bedrock of everything in the universe and people who don't have faith often do not achieve much.

The last thing that was on our minds was how to fund the business. This is contrary to the convention where money and funding usually come first but in our case. It was the last thing on our mind at the time.

At the beginning, Faustina wanted it to be only a women's magazine, but I felt that it was so narrow and suggested we make it to include men.

The next thing was deciding the content and focus. I wanted the magazine to include power of the mind. I had already opened a blog that focuses on that, but Faustina dismissed that—laughing at my naivety: "Power of the mind is not a broad and wider concept and is almost a cliche."

BRANDING

Everything has a brand! Your brand distinguishes you in the world. It is the entire experience customers have about you, products and services. Think of Coke, Ford, and Nike.

Never produce anything you don't like. If you don't love your product, then you will not respect it. Some products need to be presented. Nothing worst than presenting a product to customers and one cannot confidently present or explain them. Just as we are fearfully and wonderfully made by God. After creating humans, He said: They are beautiful, complete and lack nothing. He was pleased with His work. So must we be proud of our work. A friend once said: "She doesn't believe in court of public opinion." In the business of branding, public opinion is highly valuable. People buy you before they buy your products and services. Perceptions are important. This gives rise to opinions. Remember, a brand is made up of opinions and we all have opinions. Image, beliefs, values, mindsets and stereotypes can affect the price of products and services. All these shape people's interest and their willingness to commit their hard earned money, time and effort. Your products may be the best in the marketplace. Still, if people don't like you or don't trust you, then they may not buy from you. I remember a nice velvet material that was used to sow a brilliant garment in the 90s. The same material was used in making furniture. Suddenly, velvet materials became a poison when used for making clothes because people see the material as cheap, common and the demand dropped forcing the price down.

WHAT IS IN THE NAME?

One of the things we did not take for granted was a brand's name. This was because we understood the importance of our vision, purpose and mission. The more we understand ourselves, then the more we tend to Respect ourselves. This leads us into understanding others, and thereby compelling us to give the best to those whom we claim to have understood and the proof of that is to give them a good product and a product that we value. A product we have respect for, and the beginning of respect starts with name. Name is the power, liberation, independence and freedom. In fact, everything begins with a name and ends with a name. It is a name that we all fight to protect. So why do we don't give consideration to names? Character is critical in branding.

Clearly, we challenged ourselves by asking: "What is the best name that will project this image we have in our mind? A name that will be plain and simple yet communicate boldly our vision. Word that will communicate the why, the cause,value and belief.

We went through arrays of names but we settled for 'C. Hub, (Creative Hub)' C. Hub which means, centre, market, platform, assembling point for creativity.

It resonates with the values that we want to bring to the market and in the world. The name projects our content, purpose, aim and objectives.

It tells you where we are coming from and where we are going.

In choosing a name for your business, choose a name that has that backbone that can carry or shoulder all the things mentioned above. A name that could allow you the flexibility of enlarging your area of coverage. For example, when we want to create CA Awards, it was easy for to call it C. Hub awards, which means creativity award.

In forming your business name, you have to be imaginative. What message do you want to send out to your customers, clients and audience? It has to be wrapped as package so that when you are not there, the name can speak for itself. The name has to connect you with your product and services.

Also, the name has to connect your product and services to customers in a loud and clear manner. That resonates with customers. Then, you have to drag this your imagination to the earth.

WHEN DOES ONE START THEIR BUSINESS

Martin Luther King Jr. said: "Time is always ripe to do what is right."

Once you thought about the business, plan it and start your business. The thoughts of a righteous person are accurate. If the business is your purpose start it immediately don't wait. Purpose is a command of God, that is why MLK said that time is always ripe to do what is right. God can't release you into this world without making all things available. Go ahead time is ripe. Start with the money which you already have. The Lord will bless your plan and you shall be successful. This is how we began our business.

> **"Sow your seed in the morning and at evening
> let not your hands be idle..." Ecc 11:6**

It means you have to do your 9 to 5 job; you start your work from 5.00pm. "I do my job and in the evening I start my work. The job I am doing is not my work. I see my job as a way to help fund my work and keep my family going. This is necessary as your work is still growing." When your work has started to yield money, then you can leave your job and focus on your work. Your work is non-negotiable. Your work is your purpose.

DOES ONE HAVE ENOUGH TIME?

Listen to Muhammad Ali when it comes calculating the time we have on earth. He will determine how much you use in sleeping, going to parties, working and having fun. Put everything together; you have little or no time in this world.

You will never have enough time in this world. How one uses their time can determine what the future they will be. How you use time and what you do now can obviously shape your future.

God has given us power to predict our future. Our thoughts and actions of today determine our destiny. Sense of priority can leave more time in our pocket, while knowing that time is money. My aim in business is to inspire others to do things that inspire them, to bring out the best in people and to love what is difficult. Nothing is impossible.

This demonstrate how God has left enormous power in our hand. By thinking differently it can have a huge role on how our future look like. After all we are just 'our thoughts.'

Business is about consistency and sustainability. We also aim to reduce our overhead cost. Getting down your overhead cost is crucial with compromising on the quality and authenticity of your product is the key. Social media and search engines have made it possible for smaller businesses to be effective and efficient in terms of managing resources. Demonstrating value for money remains the strength of a small business.

WHO IS MY TARGET AUDIENCE

These are the people you want to consume your product.

What is the profile of the target audience? How are they going to be classified through demographics? What is the purchasing power?

What are their social circumstances? The segment of people to choose. One should look at this deeply in order to extrapolate with a reasonable accuracy. Get people who would love to buy your product at the same time, have disposable income to do that. You need to use your head now rather than your heart. With social media in control these days, the broad-brush appeal to social class age and income has changed a lot. You can't afford to be complacent about this as social media habit has changed the dynamics of everything now.

The Unique Selling Point – USP

This relates to authenticity and originality of an idea. What makes you different from other competitors: what makes you stand out, your uniqueness.

Your why, cause, and beliefs. This is what connects your product to the customers. This is where loyalty and trust originate. It connects your brand to you and the world. This is why you have to Respect your product and services. *Whoever buys your product and service is buying your vision.*

PRODUCT LAUNCH

"It is not what happens to you but how you react to it."
When we concluded that we were going to print the magazine, we realised how difficult it was to get good distributors. We were naive to think that we could do a huge project without securing distributors. Though we had a plan, it was not far reaching enough.

The launch was one of the most shambolic events we have ever organised. What saved the situation more was the huge downpour that I had not witnessed in the UK. Rain is a good sign, but nobody perceived such a heavy one. One of the people that saw it differently was my aunt that came from Bedford. I told her that it was a blessing because it prevented those invitees who were not truly determined to come. It saved us from their chattering. My friend, George Oparaeche, who had cancer was able to make it. It was my last sighting of him, for me he came to say goodbye.

One thing I learnt from launching is that it provides a perfect opportunity to evaluate your product and to test the market. Few people that came were amazed by the design and content of the magazine. The feedback was positive, we produced a high quality product that was outstanding. It made us different sending out our vision and destination. The saddest thing was that the turnout was poor, indicating to us the area we need to work on. Everything came down right on our face. We were not under any illusion that it would be an uphill task. What lies ahead was bigger than we thought. That day I saw the length and breadth of the ocean in the world. The scales fell off my eyes and saw we are all alone in the big ocean of business. It came to me that you sink if you stop swinging your legs. You've got to have a powerful mind to coordinate and determine the right course of your destination. For all directions look similar north and south, east and west. You've got to make the choice of direction that you intend to follow. You are now that captain and the architect of your fate. You have to take full responsibility. I thank God we started with no money. If we had had more money, then we would have spent huge amount of money that would have crippled us more.

One thing I observed about business is the experience. If you started it with little money you are better off. If we had had huge money at our disposal, we would have ran into debts. That would have made starting the business counterproductive. Most people that fail in business the first year is a result of bad advice and expectation. As a new person in business, who just went into it without experience, it is natural to think that your rate of return is equal to the amount of money you invested. Anybody that gives you advice you take it on board, due to high expectation. I don't want to call it gullibility. You don't have to be gullible, otherwise you will be subject to manipulation. You have to weigh all the advice, see if it matches with your expectations as an entrepreneur. You've got to use your heart and mind; measure each piece of advice, especially when it comes to money. How it sounds is not how it tastes. Your power of continuity is dependent on your cashflow. People are wise and they could interpret you perfectly by reading your body language. If you are broke, then they will avoid you. So make sure you have cash flow.

This is why you should be able to calculate when you start making return on investment. This is critical. If you don't know when you will start making return from sales; never start that business because people are always suspicious of new products and a new CEO. Our budget was low, so we could not launch our magazine at a posh place. Rather, we chose old kent road. With hindsight, I learnt that our decision was the best. But then I wished we had it at other beautiful venues like the places where we do events now. When one of our acquaintances said there were mistakes in our work, and we should not have any errors. Faustina told her, "If you start a new business, and your product immediately becomes error free, then on what do you have to improve?"

In Albert Einstein's words: "The person who never made a mistake never tried something new."

You can see personal circumstances are no longer an impediment.

Don't say, I don't have money. Don't say, I don't have experience. Your background is God. Your background is not the physical things you see around you. You are rich both in experience and wealth. You can launch yourself from anywhere at anytime, regardless of money or experience.

This is the knowledge and power that compelled us to start our business. "No one that holds plough and looks back worths a salt."

Remember, it is not where you are from rather where you are going that counts.

Life is about preparation – the greatest tragedy is for one to find himself unprepared and qualified for that special moment for which he was designed and tapped on by God.

If one starts a business on what he is talented at and passionate about, then you never lose. You either win or learn. You only fail when you quit.

Let the area of the business you wish to start be driven by your talent, passion and values. Don't be trapped by your fears and lack of self-confidence.

We found a gap in the market somewhere between how the stories of Africans are not properly told in the global media. To maintain the dignity and heritage of Africa and Africans, something had to be done, this means a problem has been defined. Once we identified the problem, we launched C. Hub Magazine with a vision to deal with the issues that worried us on how African identity was being represented.

First step is to know your desired outcome: Vision

Second step is to take action: Start to move towards your goal. To achieve this, you have to move to engage in actions that you clearly believe will take you in the right direction. This is important if one wants to embark on a journey. One has to face the direction of his destination.

Third step: Know what is working and what is not working for you.

If something is not working, then think what you can do. What is a logical step? Of course, it must be a change.

Fourth step: Change your approach.

We must not see adaptability and flexibility as weaknesses. Look at the lion. It is highly adaptable and flexible in its tactics but not weak. It cannot abandon its goal of not eating grass.

No amount of frustration, obstacle or challenge that will make lion eat grass. Your purpose is fixed.

Darwin: It is not the strongest, nor the most intelligent, but most adaptable.

Business is like a child. You have to nurture it and care for it.

The first is a good farmer who knows it is the time of harvest.

"Going straight ahead is always dead easy. It's absolutely a beautiful thing to do." This is what my dad told me. This is loaded; it means being focused and courageous.

In my tribe, there is a saying: 'If a king becomes too troublesome, one masks himself with a basket and talks to him.' On one cold and windy evening, we decided to wash all our dirty clothes using a washing machine. As the machine finished one set, we packed into the machine another set, later we had a pile of washed clothes that were not dried. The build up became huge because of the treacherous weather condition. One could not afford to hang clothes outside. Each time I came to check on the machine to remove the washed clothes, I was saddled by the washed clothes hipped in the lobby. I called them the mountain; they stared right on my face, menacing me, creating an illusion in my mind that lion was out there to devour whoever goes outside to spread the clothes. This is another Goliath standing tall charging and cursing me, bringing fear into my life and perhaps challenging my family.

All of us in the house; myself and my children were seeing it going around it without facing it head on. It got to a point, facing this enemy that was threatening me and my household. I went upstairs put on my track suit, sneakers and head gear. My kids asked me: 'Daddy, where are you going?' I kept my silence. Faustina didn't say anything; rather, she observed what she thought was a strange move. I'm sure she was thinking 'What is this man up to this evening?' Before they knew what was going on, I had grabbed the 'Jerks' without any apologies and pulled them out of my way to the corridor to assault them. I dealt with them one after another. In few minutes, I got all of them hung out and left them to dry. I was shocked and perplexed as my contract manager, Brian Maclean would say. The lion and tigers were nowhere to be seen. I was the only one happily prowling and strutting on the edges of the corridor looking for more clothes to spread out. What an adventure to embark on!

This is practically how we took on the world of business; brace up without turning up noses to challenge the obstacles and fears that have held us hostage since we came to England. With this principle, you can take on any challenge in your life be it; starting a business, changing career, dealing with health problems or beginning a new relationship.

The foundation on which to start your business should be on areas of your talent, because no matter how the wind and storm blows across the business world you will be strong to weather the storm. Reading and writing is my thing, so publishing is my area. Quite comfortable with that. I don't need an extra school for me to move on.

Feel comfortable in your skin! Hold yourself with pride, and let your daily actions and direction of your life be congruent with who you are.

***Where the spirit does not work with the hand, there is no art.'* Da Vinci**

Simply not applying your knowledge and understanding is the worst thing that can happen to anyone.

The decision we took to start up our publishing business without both of us having any experience, skills and money inspired me to write this: " The Big R of a successful business."

The difference between a goal and a dream is deadline, said Steve Smith.

There is nothing more exciting than to start and run your own business. Apart from profits you make, it gives you that freedom. Profits are better than wages.

I love my business so much that I see all the wonders of the world through it.

I recently had a conversation with a friend who asked me: "How did we start?" Sharing this with him.

I dutifully admire people who are frank and honest with themselves. I know there is nothing a man sets in his heart and mind that he cannot achieve. And I will admit that I did not jump into publication for the sake of filling the space. I have always had 'passion' for reading books and magazines. I am lucky to have a wife with a similar thought pattern on this issue; fear of not succeeding was not an option. We were meant to do feasibility studies, marketing research and keeping money for the rainy day. The paperwork was so staggering. I realise what Steve Jobs and Henry Ford meant:

"It is not the duty of customers to know what they want."

"If ask the customer what they want, they say faster horses."

First, I was confident that people will love our product and everything in life could be sold. All depends on strategy, passion and meaning you give your product and services to your customers. I remembered that: "We are what we are thinking." If your gut feeling says success, then it's success. If it says failure, then its failure. I could go on trying to work out this, but in the end if you conceive that you must deliver.

Without the usual business plan, I would say that we decided to turn things on its head. Act first and reflect later. Planning everything meticulously without experience and money was damn frightening.

We narrow things down.

With this strength of beliefs we launched our brand. As I look around today with humility, my beloved wife and I can say that we have joy and happiness.

"No one who holds the plough and look back worths a salt.'I, therefore, focus on the finishing line, — our vision.

Holding yourself back from what you love doing is self-harming. You must have RESPECT for yourself; not doing anything is pure ignorance.

I'm not a perfect person, as "perfection is the enemy of success." It's shameful that people I meet everyday tend to have a wrong impression of me. I do tell them to not box me in. If you do, then I will confidently wriggle out. I do take risks, whether it's not unnecessary one but a calculated one. I will always advise people to defer their judgement.

Launching a brand with little or no skill in publishing was a disaster for some people, but for me it wasn't and I did not panic. Emotional and financial well being are linked, but I separated them. Emotionally, I show maturity. I don't feel vulnerable and I don't need anyone to share instinct and thoughts now. At this critical time, one has the tendency to be swayed up and down by the public and friends. Rather I looked into the 'seed' of oneself for clues or explanations.

Prior to launching the product, I had an opportunity of setting simple objectives. I saw how possible and easy it was to accomplish them. On several occasions I had to put the interest of my business above my personal interest. This is vital, because without personal sacrifices, you won't even have a head start. This is the area where, if you don't know your purpose, vision and mission then there will be clash of interest. You have to align your beliefs, image and your thoughts with your purpose and vision. Things falter when your goal and vision vary. If you don't understand yourself, then you can be happy and successful.

I learnt that one is connected to his brand, product and services as a mum is connected to her baby. The product was as brilliant and alive as anything else. I could feel it pulsating; people who looked and flipped through the magazine were so pleased with what they saw. They reflected our values and independence; the contents and prints were done beautifully down to the smallest letter.

As much as the products are of good quality, you can't really know how the public will receive them. It's said the taste of the pudding is in the eating.

Guess what? When it was first rolled out, the public snubbed them. Friends laughed and jeered. Life does not care. It was difficult. I said to myself: we are probably not alone in this boat of starting a business. Again I said: What's the matter? Is it that everybody worry about money?

We're meant to be jubilating for the brand well-conceived and delivered— given the passion, enthusiasm and excitement. The feedback, in terms of re-turn and sales, was poor. There was instinct to slack off or give in. Something was kicking in—loss in confidence, self scrutiny and doubts all hanging around me and was brewing to a huge cloud. A friend once said: 'I know my specie.' I know the responses are disappointing, but I'm better off. What was my position before the launch of the product? I was flatlined, broke and with little option. Thinking this brought my past bare in front of me.

Thinking deeply: What have we got wrong? All I know is that quitting is off the course. The expectation was not met and the feedback was poor. The resources affected the outcome, but were not depleted.

A wiser voice says, since I had poor feedback, we should embark on a more serious sales strategy. I looked, again, at the following:

- target audience – 30 to 50 with a good disposable income of 0.6%.
- the age group.
- Gender.
- our location.
- the message.
- accessibility.

Everything seemed to have fallen into place, except the message. It was not properly communicated. The message we left out. There wasn't a direct and clear one. It was certainly not how we would like people to see us. The im-pression we want people to have about us is that of:

- Authenticity
- Reliability
- Creativity
- Innovation

Spreading the word is critical in business. Social media has become so important in our lives today that it's the revolving door through which we can effectively position ourselves and sell our products and services to the public. Had it not been for social media, we would have found it impossible to get our message across to a huge audience.

The first and best salesperson of any product is the producer: The producer knows his product more than any member of the team. This is the reason you see people like Richard Branson, Steve Jobs often appeared and played prominent role in their brand promotion. Perhaps what is true for magazine production is true elsewhere.

Be honest about the difficulties which you are facing, demonstrating your confidence in the future and in your people.

You have to talk to yourself, and make a decision to start your business . Do not talk to people on the same level with you. They are the system; they don't have anything tell you. Because they are trapped in the system with you, they got nothing to give you but discouragement and envy. You want to be bigger than them. If you need to talk to someone, the person has to be a person higher than you or an expert in what you want to do.

Remember success comes against odds.

All success starts from the mind.

My friend David once told me how he got admission into a higher institution in Nigeria. His story illustrates how all success starts from the mind.

According to him, after thinking days and months on how to gain admission into a reputable school. He decided to use his inner power without doubt.

He said: "I told myself that I'm gonna go to this school today and the first person, my inner voice tells me to talk to about admission would be the one to help me."

So, he set out from his village, which was about a 6 hour journey on a car. He was mindful of his plan and did not disclose it to anyone. He had no doubt about what he had in mind.

With that unshakeable belief, he arrived at the school, went to their campus.

He stood at their convocation arena where students were coming to see their results. He kept monitoring the students as they giggled and creaked about their results.

He saw this young man and instantly his mind clicked: "This is the man." He spontaneously called on him. "Hi, my name David. I want you to help me with admission into this school."

He said the guy's name was Peter, and immediately he stepped back in amazement.

David said: "I saw the truth in Peter's eyes."

Peter took him to a staff at the Bursary Department, there they examined David's credentials and was satisfied that he met the admission requirement. The staff told him to come back after two weeks. After two weeks, David went back to the school; straight to the bursary department. The bursary staff asked him to check the admission list at the same convocation ground and to his amazement, he saw his name as the third person on the list in his chosen department.

What you need: VISION + SKILLS + PASSION

Vision is about the direction you want to go. You require skills to produce your products, market and sell them profitably.

Passion is crucial. You should go to a job or career that provides a deep sense of purpose and meaning. Reflecting your values, passions and personality. Doing what comes naturally. What makes you become yourself.

RESPONDING TO YOUR MARKETS: FEEDBACK

Understanding time and season is crucial if you must deliver the best product or service to the customer. It essential to not go against the flow of market forces. It has been three years since we introduced our product to the market. It has not been easy, but it's worthwhile and amazing. You cannot rest on your laurels; you've got to compete with your famous rivals. Understand why they are still in business growing bigger and bigger.

Meeting your customers face-to-face is important for the continuous development of your products. The feedback I had from my customers play a role in our response to the markets. The feedback includes covering events like parties, weddings, and other ceremonies. These changed the direction of which we were heading.

At the initial time, we did not want to go into those areas. We were strictly on creativity and innovation. But the dynamics of market are changing rapidly. We needed to change the set of sail; otherwise, we could be blown out off course.

UNDERSTANDING YOUR SEASON

It didn't take long until we ran into difficulty after going into the publishing business without experience. The cost and demand for distribution went outside the curve. It became necessary to do something if we had to be in business. It calls for us to go to the drawing board to see what we were not getting right. The distributors were demanding more and more copies. The cost of printing and design was huge on us, but the sales were not matching the demand the distributors are putting on us. This was a real panic, how are we going to keep up to this demand and still have fund to be in business? We thought this distributor is going to liquidate us if we don't do something now.

We decided to limit the physical quantity of our products in circulation, while we increased our presence online. This is a digital season; there is no point going against the tide. We need to embrace the positive changes on our shores, instead of blocking the movement of tides at the high sea. It is a waste of resources and time.

Looking after your staff can reduce absenteeism. Sometimes wages account for a much higher proportion of total costs, and that is a problem when a business is at its early stage.

Strategy: Cash flow is vital in the life of a business. Business is about consistency, continuity and visibility. How can you ensure these factors are maintained if there is no cash flow? Cash flow is a live line of every business. One of the ways to ensure cash flow in business is to be wise in terms of your expenditure. If one is not careful, he ends up burning out. It is like a burner with oil; the best way to ensure that flame is constantly on is to reduce the rate at which the flame is burning. Instead of allowing a full-blown flame burning rapidly, one can drastically reduce their expenses by cutting down on overhead costs. You have to be strategic in terms of who you want to hire and why you want to hire them. Ask yourself is this essential? Is it what you can do without? Is there no alternative? And, if you decide to hire them, is the person the right person? And for how long? These questions have to be going on in your mind. Business is about a decision and process. Your ability to take a right decision will determine where you are going.

CASE STUDY

Let's look at this scenario. You are a young publisher like me. You have a book to publish. You have completed the research and discovered the book may not be an instant bestseller. You have a proposal from the printers that printing 2000 copies will cost you £2000.00; printing 5000 copies will cost you £2,799.89; and, printing 50 copies will cost you £350.00. As a young publisher, with little cash flow, that the book is still in its prime. I will go for 50 copies at £350 because I don't want to tie down my cash in printing of 5000 copies at £2,799.89. it makes business sense to conserve your running cash to be able to manage all aspects of your business.

THE GOLDEN RULE

1. **INDECISION:** This is self-doubt; no one who holds plough. When you put your heart into doing something and you don't look back. It might look hard and frightening at the beginning, but you will always emerge successful. You remember a man who was asked to change the political landscape. On getting to that political arena, he was changed by the very political landscape he was meant to change. You're meant to bring in a positive change and shape the future, but don't allow the future to shape you. Don't lose sight of your vision. Rationalise the situation. And ask yourself, "If not now, then when?" Fear is the only thing that stops you from achieving what you want. This can only stop you from reaching your goal and unlocking your potentials.

2. **YOUR FIRST PURPOSE OF STARTING A BUSINESS SHOULD NOT BE TO MAKE MONEY:** Solomon never made money his first

request. Money is a means, not an end. Money is a clay in the hand of a porter. He needs clay to make his products. We need money to achieve the result we want.

3. **PASSION:** There is no need to go into an area that you are not interested. You have to be a prisoner of your own success. Passion is powerful. In a time of difficulty, passion keeps you going beyond.

4. **YOU MUST KNOW WHEN YOUR BUSINESS WILL START MAKING RETURNS BEFORE YOU START:** If you want to build a house, then you should have a thought and reflection about it before you start. You must be willing to sustain your business as long as it takes before you make the first step. NEVER START WITHOUT SEEING THE END. You must have a vision before you start. This is why passion is critical.

5. **PRIORITIES:** Resources are scarce and the ability to prioritise them is critical towards achieving your vision.

6. **START IT LIKE A GRAIN:** If you start it little by little, and learn as you grow, then it is better than starting it with a big bang! Beginning huge, without seeing it to the end, is as well a bad beginning.

7. **KEEP YOUR OVERHEAD COST LOW:** You must reduce the amount you are pumping into the business.

8. **NEVER QUIT:** You must have a thick skin and be resilient. You should aim at finishing what you started. Fish cannot stop swimming, birds cannot stop flying. Trees cannot stop growing in the soil. Remember: it is finished by Jesus Christ. Business is not for the faint-hearted.

9. **UNDERSTANDING THE RISKS AND REWARDS OF SOCIAL MEDIA:** This is for building and retaining a competitive advantage.

10. **DO NOT LIVE IN A COCOON:** You need to interact with others and know what is happening outside your comfort zone. If you get too comfortable, and you do not evolve and improve continually, then you will be left behind. You will become outdated. You are vulnerable and defenceless if you live in a cocoon.

11. **Be Clever, Be Shrewd.** Our Lord says that you have to be as wise as a serpent and innocent as a dove. Stay on your toes at all times. For business shrewd means being wise.

12. **Be Proactive with decision making:** Correctly define a problem and identify its root cause. Don't work on its symptoms. Then, generate a solution.
13. Start small and think big.
14. **Be Unique and stand out:** Your desire to be like everyone will only hold you back. As an agent of change, you can't please everyone.

MOTIVATION VS COMMITMENT

Motivation is emotionally driven. It is a feeling based emotion. Motivation generally happens when there is a great reward to gain, or when you are suffering so badly that you want things to change. Motivation is helpful to drive you, but it is not essential to success. It is unrealistic to expect to feel motivated every day, no matter what you are doing. The problem with motivation is that it works on feeling from the emotion and these can shift very quickly.

Commitment on the other hand, comes from deep desire and discipline to achieve a set goal. For example, a surgeon can't say half way through the operation. 'Do you know I just don't feel motivated to finish this, so I'll stop now! Motivation does not matter, it is commitment that will finish the operation.

Key point

When you decide to do something, remind yourself that it is commitment (and not motivation) that matters. You've got to be transformed if you want to succeed, because you will be tested with fire. If you are not transformed, you fail the test.

PRINCIPLES OF PROBLEM SOLVING.

It is time to start thinking differently about everything. Let's look at this powerful line:
"Your way is not my way," said The Lord.
This is loaded and has given us a clue on how to solve a problem.
There are two ways: Your way and My way.

You can conceptualize in two boxes: Box A and Box B.

Don't forget that every word is nothing but a signpost: pointing the way back to the source.

Human Mind-set   God's Mind-set

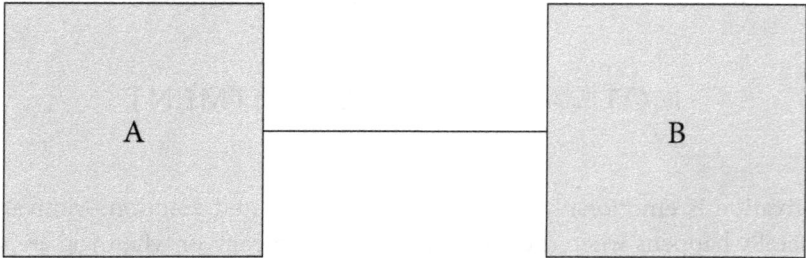

You can't solve a problem on the same platform on which it was created, according to Albert Einstein

Picture Box A as one's mindset when they have problems to solve.

Box B when one moves/Shifts his mind to a location where a solution is found. Box A is an Illusion; a place of control. The situation that is controlled is the environment. You are vulnerable in Box A. As soon as you perceive a problem, it goes into our subconscious. You stored it without realizing it.

There was a day we did not have shower gel at home. Before time came for me to bathe, Faustina had already bought one but I did not know. It had already stored in my mind: "No shower gel." Then, I proceed to the bathroom to have my shower—even though the shower gel had been placed on the bathtub, where it was highly visible, I still did not see it. When the time came for me to dry my body, my wife came in and immediately I told her," "No shower gel." There was shower gel, to my astonishment, but I did not see it because I had stored in my unconscious that there was none. At that point, I was in Box A; an illusion box. A story that there was no shower gel. It was Faustina who pointed to me: "See, shower gel here." By pointing her fingers to position of the shower gel, she had moved my mindset from Box A to Box B. In this way, the problem was solved.

In a similar way, a beggar who had been sitting by the side of the road for more than 20 years saw a stranger passed by asked: "Spare me some change?" But the stranger told him, "I have nothing to give to you." The stranger then asked the man: "What is it that you are sitting on?" The beggar answered, " Nothing. Just an old box, I have sat on for more than 20yrs." The stranger asked him: "Have you ever looked into the box?" "No." replied the beggar. "No point." Persuading the beggar to have a look inside, he agreed; and, to his surprise, there were gold inside the box that he sat for more than 20 yrs. Conditioning has made the beggar to live in that state for more than 20yrs.

"If you want to solve a problem, you have to look beyond your present circumstance."

The lesson here was that the beggar sold to himself an illusion that he had nothing for more than 20yrs. He had dwelled on that mindset. He has been in Box A for ages. It was the stranger who moved him from the mindset of nothing to a mindset of plenty. We always to sell illusions to ourselves that we have nothing. We end up believing it, and forever we get stuck in this narrative. Thereby, we find ourselves in Box A.

A man was given a punishment for escaping from prison. He was asked to dig over a big field with a spade and pitchfork. According to him, the size of the area he had to dig was meant to overwhelm him. It was meant to break his will power; defeat him and to make sure he fails. Instead of getting stuck at Box A: the big field, ie he did not allow the challenge to control him. Rather, he did allow it to limit him while allowing that environment to mess up his mind. He did not allow his situation to control him. He simply shifted his mind to Box B. This is a way to look at the bright side of things. While at box B, he became inspired and found the solution to this task. According to him, he spent the first hour coming up with concept of 3%: dividing the field into small squares.

Just Jesus fed 4,000 and 5,000 people. The miracles were ways of teaching us that we can move from the mindset of "having nothing" to a mindset of plenty. When you dwell on the mindset of nothing like the Apostles did, Jesus moved them to a new mindset of having plenty which is in box B. He practically taught them the mindset of God.

Another way you can understand this is through problem solving techniques. Let's visit the famous nine-dot puzzle.

● ● ●
● ● ●
● ● ●

Usually, you were asked to join all the nine points or dots with four straight line. One goes straight to join the nine dots to have a square. This is trap for novice. If one focus on this 9 dots without shifting paradigm, then you will never get solution. One keeps repeating it unsuccessfully, because it limited himself to the square. It is like focusing on Box A. There will be no solution. To have a solution, you have move your paradigm to box B. At B, you now realise you can extend the line a bit. Once you move your mind in this way, you get the solution. You can now connect the dots with only four lines, otherwise it is impossible. You have to think outside the box. Operate outside the dots.

If you look at Solomon's case with the harlots, it was literally impossible to know who had the baby. What Solomon applied was to have a different mindset, move to a new mindset and a new strategy. He pretended to kill the baby. In that situation, the two women gave different accounts, and one of them betrayed what was false in her.

There was another case on which a robber was detained and interrogated; he refused to confess. But when a new mindset was applied, a positive result was received. The police took another robber and pretended to have shot that one; it was only then the culprit confessed.

"If you want to solve a problem, you have to look beyond your present circumstance."

An eagle does not fight the snake in the water, which is box A. It takes the snake to the air which is box B. In the air, the snake has no power. Let box A become your present circumstance. In this situation, you can't solve your problems there. It is only resolved beyond your present circumstance, which is at Box B. To illustrate this: I had a friend who was studying physiotherapy in a university Nigeria. In those days, the course was not lucrative; my friend was very good at the course. It came to his understanding a problem he would face after graduation, so he decided to change the course

Let's say you are in the business of producing X. By producing that product, you have automatically created a problem. This will land one in Box A. At least one has spent money in producing that material. There's a problem to sell your product, to recover your money, improve on your product, or out-perform your competitors.

As you find yourself in box A, you cannot find the solution in this platform. Trying to find solution in Box A is like doing the same thing over and over again while expecting a different result. It is a rat race. Focusing on Box A is a disaster. You've got to focus on Box B. I call box A the adult's mindset; then, box B the baby's mindset.

To find a solution to the problem, you've got to move to platform B. This is where the solution is found. It is like day and night. They say if you want to drive away darkness then you must use light.

Box B is where you get the light. It is where the solution to the problem resides. Box B may be like forming a new business, attending conferences, or going out to interact with others. It's similar to meeting people and choosing to explore options through hands-on experience. Imagination is able to have fun. In this area, you are likely to get clues and cues on how to solve the problem in platform A.

This is a place of a window of opportunity. You can gain knowledge that solves that problem. To your surprise this platform will open your eyes. It is like changing another strategy. It is like changing the rules of the game like in the case of David and Goliath. Goliath was trapped in box A, while David cruised in Box B. When you move to another box, you've now altered the game plan. If you don't move to box B, then you will be glued to Box A. You gonna be there forever without solving your problems. This is the way to be in control. It also means going in a different direction. Going the counter current.

You will never solve your problem in box A. You've got to focus on box B. The real solution is in Box B and not the in Box A. It is like solving human ailment; you focus on the skin. You've got to go to the root, and so you've got to go the mind.

Problem and solution cannot be in the same box. It follows this natural phenomenon of night and day. Neither light nor darkness live in a room. Fullness and emptiness cannot be inside a box.

Two brothers: one is chosen and one is rejected. It's like spirit and body. The principle of problem solving has opened another way for the third book; "Abraham Leave Your Home."

One day I asked Faustina a question about her great uncle, Chief C. N Nwagwu, former Executive Director operations Central bank of Nigeria. That question prompted us to begin a search about him on Google. We searched three times with his titles and nothing substantial showed up. At this point Faustina changed the search keywords combining various mixes

. Until she searched for books on banking in his name, only then did his name show up. Had she dwelled in the first search, using the title that failed, then she would have been stuck in what I called box A. It was doing the same thing over and over and expecting a different result. When that did not produce the result she moved to Box B. She changed the theme of her search, instantly getting what she wanted.

We will either find a way or we will make one. **Hannibal**

IMPORTANT EXTRAS

If you do not see the value of social media, you will never benefit from it.
Faustina Anyanwu

It can never be overstated. Social media remains one of the most valuable things that's happened to this generation. As the world population expands, there is more need for a global market. There's social media to offer that global shopping malls. We now have a world beyond borders.

Social media provides immeasurable income streaming opportunities for people, yet people moan and complain of how horrible social media is. When I meet such people, I usually listen carefully and then ask them several questions to understand where their worries lie. Unfortunately, the majority give answers like: 'Oh, people are just showing off there.' ' There's a lot of negative things on social media.' 'How can one put all about their lives on social media?' 'There's a lot of fraudsters on social media.' Oh, I want my privacy.' The list goes on and on.

When they're done with their litany of why and how social media is a bad idea, I usually will respond with the following questions: – Would you stop living because your neighbour or people living in your area are showing off their wealth? When you know an area in your neighbourhood has some baddies what do you do? Do you not avoid taking that route? Or, you stop going out at all so you don't have to see them? In real life, do you not do things to meet your privacy or personality needs? When you go to the market do you not see different kinds of people selling, yelling and beckoning on you to buy from them? Don't you see shops trying their best to attract your attention? Don't you often go to the market or shops for window shopping? If you answered yes to any of the above, then you've been browsing social media with your legs without knowing it.

By the time I'm done with my many questions, their mouth would be left wide open without any reasonable words coming out of it. Social media offers as much, if not more and greater opportunities, as real life. As many as you worry of social media, I will be addressing each of them one by one later. But now let's talk about the many benefits you may be losing out from because of your apathy for social media.

Whether you're on social media as an entrepreneur, or as a window shopper, —there are so many benefits to embrace. From information to meeting new people and networking, Social media has as much chances for you as you would in real time.

Socialisation : Social media has reconnected me with so many of my classmates for whom I may never have seen again in life. From time to time, we catch up on both our times in school and where we are today. Gives you opportunity to truly evaluate your progress in comparison to your performance. So many people have discovered their long lost relatives, reunited and now are in close contact with each other. More beneficial is to most descendants of slaves, who are now able to trace and are connecting better with people of their roots. Information is now passed on so quickly, raising awareness and helping people discover facts of which they never knew. For instance, years back the only information people in Africa had of the Western World was only what was shown to them on televisions , radios and or magazines. Unknowing to them that those information went through heavy editorial processes, protecting the image of supremacy. While, for those in the Western World, the only knowledge they knew of Africa or Asia was the exact propaganda their traditional media showed them.

It is the long period of these misinformation that created so much gap between races, interactions and integration. Some have been brain-washed for so long that they are superior to others while some believe they are less superior. Contrary to that, social media in the last half a decade, have opened up more channels for people to access a more accurate information—especially in terms of human diversity and existence.

Business: Social media offers a vast marketplace for global shoppers. Services, products, companies are connected in a split second. However, only the 'smartest' gets to snap up these opportunities. More and more start-ups have been able to take off within a short time with the help of social media. Ideas are flowing for free and the 'smartest' are also grabbing those ideas. They are turning them to real time money with streaming ventures on social media. For someone like me, owning a publishing company may have been a dream that I will never wake up to in my life. There are waves of different kinds of people actualising their dreams of being self employed, earning a decent living and having enough time to still do what they love doing. Women are the greatest beneficiaries of social media business benefits, as more women can now conveniently run their business from their kitchen table, do their school runs, take care of the family and still be a financially contributing part to the economy. Services are now more accessible and cheaper with more and more people competing for the jobs available in the world virtual market. Opportunities are no longer in the hands of few who decide who gets those opportunities. Rather, more people are taking time to create their own opportunities—using social media to source their market and working with people from around the world. They don't have to move to an unknown or unwelcoming geographic region

Statistics: As of January 2015, 7.2 billion people in the world, 1.4 billion are Facebook users, 284 million are active twitter users , there are 363 million Google+ users, Linkedin has 347 million generating revenue in excess of $643 million at the end of 2014, (a growth rate of 44% over the previous period). The figures are only going up everyday getting the smartest people smarter by day and by revenue. **Source:** wearesocial.net

Still in doubt of social media benefits?

Think of communication difficulties 10 years ago. Now, think of today when all you have is the internet to connect with anyone. Think of Skype, Facebook messenger, Whatsapp, BBM, Viber and many more. There are magazines, TV, radio stations and news accessible in real-time, mostly for free to people in different parts of the world. Social media has got to a point where it can no longer be ignored. Risk ignoring it and see yourself disappear into the vacuum which you've created.

Are there any bad tastes to social media?

Of course, there's this world filled with living things. As long as there's life, one faces risks everyday. You wouldn't because of risks stop living. Social media is now part of life. If you still wish to participate and remain relevant to that life, then you have to discover your coping strategy to snap up the opportunities before you to be part of the game.

For each risk you're worried about, there's a remedy.

Discover the best social media platform that resonates with your personality, your business, your message or your general view about life. For example, If you want to have active pictorial interactions, then connect with friends on Facebook. Catch fun, as well as reach a general market for your business. Linkedin is a platform for serious-minded professionals and entrepreneurs. Although, over time, it's beginning to relax it's serious nature.

Twitter offers opportunity for you to air your views without being unnecessarily interactive with strangers. Instagram gives you an opportunity to visually share your activities, attracting like minds together. Pinterest gives you the opportunity to discover your inner self by offering you the platform to collect things that truly interest you. Your collection of pins can be a great pointer to discovering yourself and for people to discover your interest. There are many platforms to discover for a start. Make use of the buttons on any of the platforms you choose. Each of the platforms has a great deal of options for you to control what comes to you and what goes out to whom.

The best advice, however, is this: "Do not share on the internet anything you do not want anyone else to see or know about you." There are various privacy settings, both for blocking or unfriending those you dime intrusive or rude. On Facebook, you can unfollow updates, people, groups and or any advertisements. You can also have yourself untagged from pictures or updates. You generally have control over what you see on social media. Again, in real life there are several things you cannot avoid seeing.

Fraudsters: If you would walk into a shop and trust your laptop to a total stranger, then why do you think it's any different from doing business with others over the internet or social media? It's straightforward. If it doesn't seem right, then it's probably not right. Ask for referrals and reviews. Check who has used what services and what are their experiences. And always trust your gut instinct, just as you would in real life. Social media is only an extension of your average market or shopping mall. If you don't give your money in exchange for service in a market, then why do so on social media? If you wouldn't chat with a total stranger on the street, then why chat with strangers online? If you wouldn't go into a porn shop in real life, then why check into a porn site on the internet? If you won't leave your house unlocked, then why leave your social media accessible to all? It's really you who isn't growing to adjust with the time. Why not find ways to figure it out before the ground caves in underneath your feet.

Truly, change is never an easy thing. However, this change has reached a point where it's either you be part of the change and benefit—or be changed by the wave and get swept under it. It's your choice.

SIMPLE STEPS TO TIGHTEN YOUR SOCIAL MEDIA MARKETING

By Faustina Anyanwu

Social media is one the most powerful tools available to boost visibility and engage prospects for every business this era. If not properly executed, could cause worse damage to any brand of any scale. Ability to manage your brand on social media can be tricky. These simple steps however, are all you need to work in your favour. Remember, this has got be on-going.

Target and position your small business

Before you get started in your business, you want to define who your typical client would be. So, if you already know who your target market is, then you also know where they are. Great.

However, social media is a different terrain from all other environments and factors. On social media, a person's behaviour is influenced by several other factors. Things are changing very fast. You need to understand these factors and how it's affecting your audience's behaviour. Where are they, when do they come online, and which platforms are they using? What are they responding to the most often?

Listen and observe

Every entrepreneur has a responsibility to listen to what their customers are saying about them. Especially on social media. Studies have found that negative news spread like wide fire. To be in control, you must listen and observe behaviour of your followers towards your products. Identify the influencers. These are those who are almost always online; they drive the conversation, have loyalists, and are like a passenger train that carries every other person to their destination. They have the most re-shares, likes and more. Discover who this is within your audience and make them your advocate directly or indirectly.

Engage and Interact

Having found your audience and taken your position, now is time to get to meet your audience and interact with them. Gradually, day by day, you communicate your brand's story in so many different ways. There's no one-size-fits-all here. All you have to do is discover various different ways to keep your audience hooked on your brand. Eg: Weekly prize draw, engaging articles , questions, incentives to participate in your surveys and so on. You just have to be creative, honest and keep it simple.

Protect your brand

As much as you want to engage with your audience, you want to be careful not to get trapped in a damaging encounter. Here are few ways to prevent this or ameliorate any encounter, if it ever occurs. Separate your brand from personal use; respond quickly and honestly to any negative feedbacks; apologise where necessary; and, compensate if need be. Your ultimate aim here is to prevent further damage, as negative news fly so quickly out of control on social media.

Evaluate and measure your success

This should usually be an ongoing thing. You may decide to do this daily, weekly or monthly. The smaller your business, the more often you should measure how much impact your social media presence is making in the growth of your business. Facebook has a very fantastic and easy way to help you keep an eye on what your audience is doing with your engagement with them.

For more practical workshops on startups, small business growth, social media success, join the Divas of Colour Influencers club on www.divasofcolour.com

FREQUENTLY ASKED QUESTIONS

Everyone struggles with one or two of these questions.

1. How do I balance my career with my family?
2. How do I build a career that is meaningful, joyful and fulfilling?
3. How do I start my own business?
4. How do I make a difference in the world?
5. How do find a job I love?

These are questions I answer all the time at our conferences, on my youtube channel and Facebook. What a great opportunity for you to connect with the practical ways I help entrepreneurs like you to find their vision.

Come and have conversations with others on how to make your vision commercially viable.

CONNECT WITH ME

Website: www.emekaanyanwu.co.uk
Twiter: @Venthevc
Facebook: Emeka Anyanwu.

www.ingramcontent.com/pod-product-compliance
Lightning Source LLC
Chambersburg PA
CBHW071601210326
41597CB00019B/3354